CASE STUDY METHODS

JACQUES HAMEL
with
STÉPHANE DUFOUR
DOMINIC FORTIN
Université de Montréal

Qualitative Research Methods
Volume 32

0803954166

SAGE PUBLICATIONS

International Educational and Professional Publisher
Newbury Park   London   New Delhi

For information address: *1991 pour la version française:*

 SAGE Publications, Inc.   Les Éditions Saint-Martin
2455 Teller Road   4316 boul. St-Laurent
Newbury Park, California 91320   bureau 300
                                        Montréal, Qc.
SAGE Publications Ltd.   H2W 1Z3
6 Bonhill Street
London EC2A 4PU
United Kingdom

SAGE Publications India Pvt. Ltd.
M-32 Market
Greater Kailash I
New Delhi 110 048 India

Printed in the United States of America

Library of Congress Cataloging-in-Publication Data

Hamel, Jacques, 1956-
    [Enquête de terrain en sciences sociales. English]
    Case study methods / Jacques Hamel, with Stéphane
Dufour and Dominic Fortin.
          p.   cm.   — (Qualitative research methods ; v. 32)
    Includes bibliographical references (p. 51).
    ISBN 0-8039-5415-8 (cl.)   — ISBN 0-8039-5416-6 (pbk.)
    1. Case method.   2. Social sciences—Research—Methodology.
I. Dufour, Stéphane, 1967- . II. Fortin, Dominic, 1967- .
III. Title. IV. Series.
HN62.M231813   1993
300'.722—dc20   93-26644
                                                 CIP

94 95 96 10 9 8 7 6 5 4 3 2

Sage Production Editor: Yvonne Könneker

CONTENTS

EDITORS' INTRODUCTION

Case studies are a familiar but disparate narrative form. They appear in a variety of guises, across many disciplines both basic and applied. Case studies appear in law, education, history, medicine, psychology, and administrative studies. The uses to which they are put include cultural description, professional preparation, theory construction, biographic study, clinical diagnosis, and policy analysis. Some fields it seems are built almost entirely on knowledge produced through individual, cumulative, and comparative case studies. Certainly the distinctiveness if not wonder of anthropology rests on ethnographic case studies. But anthropology is hardly alone in having a case method. In the midst of such diversity, however, is the categorical singularity of case studies. The research aim may be on describing, understanding, or explaining, but it is the focused *n*-of-one character that sets a case study apart as a method among methods.

This singularity is of course controversial. To some, case studies offer little scientific or disciplinary value. They are thought of as exploratory forays into previously unexplored territories: a kind of scouting expedition, useful (more or less) to those who possess more systematic means of defining, mapping, and understanding the conceptual terrain opened up by a case study. To others, case studies carry a good deal of scientific or disciplinary value. They are thus able to stand (or fall) on their own merits. In sociology, case studies have a long-standing pedigree that reaches back to the misty origins of the field. It is a pedigree that has been questioned, of course, and subjected to a good deal of scrutiny. But from such intense inspection has come a rather refined and sophisticated contemporary understanding of the role case studies can (and perhaps should) play within the discipline.

This provides the starting point for Jacques Hamel's treatment of *Case Study Methods* in the 32nd volume of the Sage Series on Qualitative Research Methods. In a most economical fashion, Hamel provides a practical guide for producing theoretically sharp and empirically sound sociological case studies. A central idea put forth by Hamel is that case studies must "locate the global in the local" thus making the careful selection of the research site the most critical decision in the analytic process. There is a history associated with this argument in sociology and this history is given substance in the author's useful and nearly exhaustive thematic bibliography of the case study method as presented in the appendix. Yet, as the text makes clear, this history is not an American one exclusively. French sociology as developed in the family monograph tradition of Frédéric La Play has also valuable lessons to teach.

There is much to ponder in this slim volume. Jacques Hamel not only places differing case study approaches into contrasting historical and societal contexts but puts forth his own thoughtful resolution for just how the apparent contradictions and dilemmas associated with the use of case studies in sociology can best be overcome. His aim is to show how case studies can be accomplished such that the wealth of empirical materials they typically generate will be placed within relevant and theoretically informative sociological arguments. The idea must always be "to explain the social by the social" and the object of this explanation cannot, in Hamel's view, arise from fieldwork per se but must come from the re-searcher's own distinctive point of view. How such objects can be located with sociological savvy, imagination, and clarity is very much at the heart of this monograph.

—John Van Maanen
Peter K. Manning
Marc L. Miller

ACKNOWLEDGMENTS

This work was first published in French by Éditions Saint-Martin as part of a collection from the Department of Sociology at the Université de Montréal, called *L'Enquête de terrain en sciences sociales* [Fieldwork in the social sciences]. Its appearance in a revised and substantially modified English version is the work of Professor John Van Maanen and publisher Mitch Allen. Their interest in the French edition of this book and the confidence they have shown by publishing an English version of it is much appreciated.

This book is based on a widespread interest in the qualitative methodologies of sociology and anthropology, particularly as they apply to field and case studies. These techniques have received special attention in my research and teachings at the Université de Montréal. Although I initiated the first forays into the literature on this subject, the research needed to compile this bibliography required the collaboration of two young, devoted, and enthusiastic researchers: Stéphane Dufour and Dominic Fortin. The initial plan to produce this bibliographic inventory took shape over the course of numerous conversations with these researchers, following an initial survey by Stéphane Dufour of the published literature in this field. Dominic Fortin joined him and together they worked relentlessly for two summers to complete their task. More recently, François Poisson provided an adept adaptation of this bibliography aimed at the needs of English-language readers.

I would like to express my gratitude to all those who generously assisted in the compilation of this bibliography.

Librarians Jihad Fahrat and Jerry Bull of the Bibliothèque des lettres et des sciences humaines at the Université de Montréal, provided pertinent advice and direct support to the research conducted under my direction. The patience and diligence they demonstrated, when faced with complex demands, merits our heartfelt thanks. Moreover, many items in this bibliography were included as a result of the constant assistance they provided, made all the more valuable by the depth of their professional experience.

Gilles Houle became interested in my work, and considered publishing it in the collection he was preparing, when it was still in the embryo stage. He has given his wise counsel in shaping the work, thus making it a more

viii

user-friendly text. I would like to thank him for his ideas and suggestions, always imparted in good spirits. I owe much to comments made by readers of a first draft of this manuscript. These include Léon Bernier of the Institut québécois de recherche sur la culture, Jean-Michel Chapoulie of the École normale supérieure de Saint-Cloud, Denise Couture of the Department of Sociology of the Université de Montréal, Évelyne Desbois of the CNRS in Paris, Hughes Dionne of the Université du Québec à Rimouski, Nicole Gagnon of the Department of Sociology at Université Laval, Jennifer Platt of the Sussex University, Paul Sabourin of the Department of Sociology of the Université de Montréal, Robert K. Yin of the COSMOS Corporation, and Françoise Zonabend of the Laboratory of Social Anthropology of the Collège de France. Their appraisals, which I have read and reread, have made them partners in a work that owes much to their insightful and appropriate remarks. I would like to express my gratitude to them for having devoted their time and contributed their experience.

The Directors of the Department of Sociology of the Université de Montréal, Danielle Juteau and Marcel Fournier, provided me with their support from the start of this research project. This support was substantial, as they were able to convince the authorities of the Université de Montréal and the Humanities and Social Science Research Council of Canada to provide the funding needed to set up the project and get it underway. In particular, I would like to thank them for having obtained the backing for the financial requirements of this project from Yves Murray, Miklos Zador, and Gilles Beaudet in the office of the Assistant Dean for Research at the Université de Montréal. I would also like to thank the latter for the cordial relationship we have maintained. Micheline Varin, Administrative Secretary of the Université de Montréal Department of Sociology, was of essential assistance in the immense and complicated task of typing the bibliography.

My last words of thanks should, in fact, have been my first. I would like to thank here all those who, over the past few years, have accepted the burdensome task of producing yet another version of this manuscript with exemplary patience and competence, despite the tightest deadlines. My repeated demands for impossible speed were met with quality work and good spirits by Chantal Côté, Micheline Dessurault, Lucie Lévesque, and Mireille Loiseau. I cannot thank them enough for the services they rendered, without which a work of this type could not be produced. I feel it is important to express to them my great appreciation for their support and assistance, because this work is also, in many ways, their work. Thanks, too, to Dominique Boucher for her editing of the presentation, and to Maureen Nicholson, who was responsible for the English translation.

. . . the method simultaneously expresses the subjective approach of the thinker and the objective content of what he is thinking about. In the last analysis, though, it is the content that provides the "grounds" for the method, since, while the method expresses the procedure adopted by the thought process, the latter expresses the nature of what is being thought about.

Maurice Godelier
(1972, p. 134)

CASE STUDY METHODS

JACQUES HAMEL
with
STÉPHANE DUFOUR
DOMINIC FORTIN
Université de Montréal

1. THE CASE STUDY: DIFFERING PERSPECTIVES

The origin of the term *case study* is linked to that of *case history*. The latter is widely used in clinical fields such as psychology and medicine. Sociological case studies (or their equivalent *monographic studies*) have proved to be investigations of particular cases. Such a study is conducted "by giving special attention to totalizing in the observation, reconstruction and analysis of the cases under study" (Zonabend, 1992, p. 52). Accordingly, a case study is an in-depth study of the cases under consideration, and this depth has become another feature of the case study approach.

But is the case study a method? Or is it an approach? French sociology clearly describes it as a *monographic approach*. Case studies employ various methods. These can include interviews, participant observation, and field studies. Their goals are to reconstruct and analyze a case from a sociological perspective. It would thus be more appropriate to define the case study as an approach, although the term *case method* suggests that it is indeed a method.

If the case study is an approach, it one that is driven by the desire to establish a sociological study based on a case. This poses the formidable problem of defining what its goal truly is. What are sociology and

1

sociologists trying to explain? The issue is not whether an explanation is to be produced from one or more cases. There is as yet no satisfactory answer to this question. The objectives of sociology are differently defined according to various theoretical perspectives operating within the field. Sociology may wish to study individual interactions, common patterns of behavior, and social structures; this list is far from being complete. What purpose does the case study serve under such circumstances?

As a sociological approach, the case study strives to highlight the features or attributes of social life. This is true whether the latter is perceived as a set of interactions, as common behavior patterns, or as structures. Anthropology has provided us with this definition of the case study, just as it has been responsible for establishing its acclaim. In fact, the case study had a substantial impact during its heyday on nascent American and French sociological study. A brief history of the subject will illustrate this.

Brief History of the Case Study in Anthropology and Sociology

If we were to list names and schools of thought associated with the case study, as defined in this manner, we would undoubtedly begin with Bronislaw Malinowski, Frédéric Le Play, and members of the Chicago School. The history of the case study revolves around these names. They are an appropriate starting point for becoming acquainted with its fortunes and misfortunes in sociology and anthropology. Nonetheless, the history of the rise, the fall, and then the dramatic resurgence of the case study depends on whether we are speaking of sociology or anthropology, and its French or Anglo-Saxon schools. This is what we shall try to demonstrate here.

THE CASE STUDY AND PARTICIPANT OBSERVATION: BRONISLAW MALINOWSKI

To escape World War I, Bronislaw Malinowski, a Polish-born Austrian, took refuge in Melanesia, where he lived three years in the Trobriand Islands. This forced stay quickly became an opportunity for the anthropologist-to-be to make his first observations of the local population, and what were to him its strange and exotic ways and customs. These carefully noted reflections were to appear in a series of famous works, including *Argonauts of the Western Pacific* (1922/1953).

Malinowski's fieldwork was what gave rise to modern anthropology, where participant observation made its first foothold. In keeping with the anthropological thinking of the time, Malinowski cataloged every detail of the society under study. For Malinowski, culture meant common patterns of behavior, beliefs, and rituals marking the life of a society in its various manifestations. Culture could certainly be understood through the attentive observation of the behavior of the actors in the society under study, and the rituals they shared. However, such observation would not, in and of itself, go far enough. The study of culture also required an understanding of the meanings actors assigned to their own patterns of behavior, beliefs, and rituals prevalent in their society. Such observation must thus be "participant," in the sense that the description of a culture requires the participation of field informants. The meaning each ascribes to such behavior can be understood through their descriptions of it. Such observation is participant, furthermore, because the observer personally takes part as an anthropologist in observed rituals and behavior patterns.

The definition of participant observation is, in the sense instituted by Malinowski, quite simple. He believed it was adequate for the observer to gradually become integrated within the local population, through regular contacts over a long period. This observer would become involved in daily life and customs, while trying not to alter them by his or her presence or through the observational process. The use of key informants, with whom close contact is maintained, makes it possible to collect remarks in situ, which could shed light on direct observations. Firsthand observations and information must be meticulously noted in field logs designed to faithfully reproduce the traits of the culture studied. The manner in which observations and information are organized in these logs obviously depends on the comments of informants and the anthropologist's initial understanding obtained in the field.

Under such circumstances, culture should be studied within local populations, small communities whose homogeneity clearly illustrates their particular traits in a consolidated manner. Villages (or tribes) proved to be ideal observation sites for culture, from this perspective. Because of their small size and homogeneity, the cultures under study appeared as macrocosms. French anthropologist Marcel Maget emphasized the benefits of the village as a place to observe culture, which he defined as the common behavior patterns, beliefs, and rituals of a social group or of a society:

The village is a favourite place for the monographic study. It is not indeed of such a size that it exceeds the absorption capacities of a single researcher who, even if he is a specialist, can have an individualized synoptic view of the whole group. The weak cultural differentiation permits comprehension of the whole range of meanings which have value in the present. (Maget, 1953, p. 57)

The village, which at the dawn of anthropology offered a homogeneous social life, combined with a low population density, immediately provided many practical benefits for case studies. This is because the village is, in itself, an "enlargement of all of the culture's traits and features" (Maget, 1953, p. 57).

In anthropology, many case studies are established from this perspective, so that one can maintain that the village possesses methodological qualities making it an ideal vantage point for getting a grasp of a culture or social life as a whole. In this way the village contains microcosmic versions of itself, each one enclosing still smaller reproductions, like a Russian doll ("babushka"), as Edmund Leach suggests:

It is assumed that a social system exists within a somewhat arbitrary geographical area; the population involved in this social system is of one culture; the social system is uniform. Hence the anthropologist can choose for himself a locality of "any convenient size" and examine in detail what goes on in this locality; from this examination he will hope to reach conclusions about the principles of organization operating in this particular locality. He then generalizes from these conclusions and writes a book about the organization of the society considered as a whole. (Leach, 1964, p. 60)

Recently, however, questions have been raised about the qualities attributed to the village by this school of thought. Today's village is no longer the strategic vantage point for perceiving the culture or social life of a modern society as a whole. The first case studies mainly concerned "small, insular societies in which individuals interacted directly and constituted real and virtually closed groups, set within geographically confined regions. Relations with external groups were few and far between" (Champagne, 1982, p. 8). Under such circumstances, culture and social life were relatively homogeneous. Not many peculiarities appeared. Such homogeneity was largely based on the order and simplicity of individual interaction. In other words, social relationships were the same on the scale of a physical location such as the village, as they were on the global scale of society itself.

The entry of these societies into the modern age, through the universalization of economic exchange, the creation of modern communication tools, and the deterritorialization of lifestyles and institutions, destroyed the homogeneity of culture or social life. Culture and social life have become so complex these days that it would be hard to claim that a culture or a society could be fully studied using the physical and geographic framework of the village alone.

THE CASE STUDY IN FRENCH SOCIOLOGY: FRÉDÉRIC LE PLAY'S FAMILY MONOGRAPHS

This issue raises the problem of how social life can be perceived as a whole, on the basis of the study of a single case. If, with modernization, the village is no longer the key, what then is the case, or the social unit, that can provide a holistic view of modern social life? Sociological case studies were devised in response to this question, among others. This is particularly so with French efforts in this field, due to the work of Frédéric Le Play. He is properly considered the founder of sociological fieldwork and of the case study in France.

Frédéric Le Play (1806-1882) was born in Rivière-Saint-Sauveur, in the Calvados region of France, near the town of Honfleur, where his father was a civil servant in the customs administration. As he would write in his key work, *Les Ouvriers européens* (1855), he spent the first years of his childhood there, "in the middle of a Christian seafaring population that was devoted to country, and sheltered from the dissenting views that had, since 1789, found their ways throughout most of the rest of France" (p. 37). Le Play's adolescence and childhood were spent in a protective, family-oriented, Christian environment.

His admission to the prestigious École Polytechnique, followed in October 1827, by acceptance at the École des Mines, was more than a mere academic success for Le Play. These events placed him squarely amid the current events of his time. Le Play was to come into contact with the forces of change in his society, and become involved in the new wave of scientific and political thought of his time. He did so without ever turning his back on his basic and very traditional training and its family-oriented, Christian, and provincial nature. It was during his years at the École des Mines that he became keenly interested in the issue of the decline and prosperity of societies, and the transition from one such state to another. This gave him the idea of founding a social science. A field trip into a mining region as part of the curriculum of the École des Mines gave him the first opportunity to do so. Accompanied by his friend and fellow student Jean Reynaud, he decided to travel through northern Germany in the summer of 1829. He certainly intended to visit mines, factories, and forests, but he also planned to study worker populations.

Le Play's studies at the École des Mines were interrupted for more than a year by an unfortunate laboratory accident. He used that time to write his travel diary. It was an outstanding work that convinced the school's administration to hire him as editor of its journal, *Annales des Mines*. This job enabled him to travel each year and continue the trips to mines he had begun with Reynaud. It also let him continue his observations of the working class. The quality of his work and the new life he infused into the *Annales des Mines* won him his first trip outside of France for this review. He went to Spain in 1833 to study the Iberian Peninsula's mineral wealth, especially its lead mines. The following year, he was appointed to the mining industry's Permanent Statistics Commission, remaining its mainstay until 1848.

Under the auspices of this commission, Le Play conducted a systematic study of the working-class populations of various European nations. In 1835 and 1836 he went to Belgium, England, Scotland, and Ireland. In 1837, his travels took him to Austria and southern Russia. This trip marked his first encounter with patriarchal societies, and these were a major revelation for Le Play. He in fact learned from such societies, where patriarchs, married sons, and their families shared the same household, that the family is the mainspring of all societies. One could therefore claim that family organization determines the type of social organization. Observing them thus helped him understand Western societies. In some ways anticipating ethnology, or for that matter, contemporary anthropology, he stated that "the example of undeveloped societies provides arguments [for the understanding of developed societies] which are all the more convincing, since the facts, freed from the complications of a highly refined society, provide the observer with greater clarity and precision" (Le Play, 1857/1983, Vol. 1, p. 123). The comparative method appeared indispensable in this context, and Le Play opted for it in the continuation of his work.

Le Play developed his method in the course of his early travels. Although the idea of going on site, into the field, as this process of observing social reality is called today, is not a new one, Le Play's originality lay in his method and in the underlying purpose of this observation. The observation involved in his approach essentially corresponds to his ambition, and to his goal, of understanding movement in societies. This movement is the alternation between prosperity and decline, and the transition from one to the other. Social peace accompanied by stability was what he meant by prosperity. This stability is not that of a static, self-sufficient society; rather, it is a stability achieved through the successful integration of material progress. This process notably results from developments in science and technology. Decadence, conversely, is the state of a society where social peace and stability are jeopardized by the fact that, for all manner of reasons, such progress has not been successfully integrated.

Le Play's method presumes that society cannot be studied as a single entity or unit. The focus must be on some key element. This element will serve as a prime observation point, one that makes up the society's basic unit. This unit will reveal the characteristic features of the society, its social state. Based on Le Play's initial observations, he concluded that the family is this observation point, or the case. An in-depth study of the family case would provide an understanding of the society in its characteristic features. He selected the working-class family as this unit. These families worked with their hands in farming and in industry, represented the largest population group, and were most easily observable. He made this selection not only for the sake of convenience, but out of the desire to generalize his findings.

Choosing the family, particularly the working-class family, was not a matter of chance or of personal preference. The family is society's unit of production and reproduction on a biological level. French society at the time was a working-class one. Thus, the working-class family permitted an in-depth study of that society, based on the assumption that the "condition of a society may be revealed through the systematic study of an appropriately selected micro-social unit" (Kalaora & Savoye, 1989, p. 46). This microsocial unit, the ideal case, was no longer for Le Play the physical location (the village). Rather, it was a social unit, intentionally selected to provide a better understanding of the characteristic traits of society as a whole.

Under Le Play's initiative, more than 300 family monographs were produced. He was personally responsible for nearly 100 of them. A precise and detailed monographic study was conducted for each working-class family, using a standardized approach. Le Play later stated that the main lines of this approach had been drawn up in 1839. It began with preliminary observations. These were described in 13 paragraphs, and listed under four headings: "definition of the location, the industrial structure, and the family," "how the family earns its living," "how the family lives," and "history of the family." The family's annual income and expenses were next determined. Great detail was given to all forms of income, as well as to expenses for food, clothing, housing, maintenance, health, and education. The meticulousness of this system was designed to ensure that preliminary observations were detailed and accurate. These monographs concluded by describing "various components of the social environment" and "key elements in the social organization." This section was designed to shed additional light on the family by placing it within its environmental context.

These monographs required on-site studies lasting from a week to a month, with observations and information meticulously collected over a long period of field study. This approach assumed that:

> The observer could explore the entire dwelling to catalogue furniture, utensils, linen and clothing, and could assess real estate, cash on hand, livestock, special equipment required for work and industry, and, generally, the family's property. Food reserves were appraised, and food used in the meals, depending on the season, was weighed. Finally, details were collected on all work performed by every family member, within and outside the household. (Le Play, 1879/1989, p. 221)

Le Play proposed "three methods which are far from equal in importance" in his *Instruction sur la méthode d'observation dite des monographies de famille* [Instructions on observational methods in family "monographs"] (1862/1882, p. 49). These methods were: observing the facts, questioning the worker on subjects that could not be directly observed, and collecting information from individuals in the community who were outside the family structure (whom he called "social authorities"). Although there was direct observation of, and communication with, the family, this was not the sole source of information. Family statements were verified by persons in the community who knew the family well. Le Play also talked with informants selected from among the local social authorities. Social authorities were informants well able to provide information on anything concerning the social organization under investigation. In Le Play's view, they were "models," ideal types, with whom he checked the conclusions of the monograph he produced on his selected working-class family case.

The working-class family monographs he and his followers produced demonstrated that many different family types existed. Le Play presented them in a "classification of family categories." This work highlighted various types of social organization, as the ideal observation site for Le Play was the family. His classification is essentially based on the family inheritance system, breaking down societies into three main groups, according to the kinds of families that make them up. These groups are: societies with patriarchal families, societies with stem families, and societies with unstable families.

The patriarchal family is distinguished by the fact that family property is left to a single heir, who is usually the eldest. The family nonetheless retains a community function. Its single members, or those living outside of the family, still rely on the community's "material and psychological resources." The community that must provide for them is the family. Family members are thus incapable of devoting "themselves to creative pursuits." They are little inclined to take the initiative, because they tend to remain within the bosom of the family. Such a family, as well as the society it serves as a foundation, is essentially conservative. This type of family, and type of society, tends to engender decadence, which compromises the social peace for which the family and the society nonetheless strive.

Inheritance rights in the stem family are normally conferred on the eldest male, or in any event a sole heir. Family assets, which are his by right, are used for his wife, to help out his siblings, and to look after his parents. By keeping the family heritage to himself, the heir contributes in reducing the community function of the family, thus forcing family members to take individual initiatives and constraining them to depend solely on themselves, while looking out for the welfare of the family. Transmission of the family heritage thus serves to enhance the enterprising spirit of family members. The family, like the rest of society, is dedicated to prosperity, a state of social peace, and stability. Since social stability is ensured by the stem family, Le Play promoted this structure as part of any social reform. Based on his family monographs, he supported a social reform in which he defended the stem family. He felt that it alone could ensure the social stability of any society.

Stem family inheritance rights run directly contrary to the Napoleonic Civil Code, which provided for an equal distribution of family assets. Furthermore, the Civil Code gave rise to a family heritage structure that would seem to have little to do with the essentially fiduciary nature of financial assets, which play such a major role in modern fortunes. By definition, the accumulation of capital runs counter to the idea of tying up capital for long periods. Capital cannot be accumulated by being frozen as in the inalienable possession of property, particularly when such property is managed to ensure the perpetuation of the heritage, rather than to provide the best possible yield from financial assets.

Le Play's favoring the right of a sole heir, usually the eldest, to inherit quickly resulted in his being labeled a reactionary. Furthermore, family monographs produced by his own supporters revealed that founding families do not necessarily ensure social stability, nor the society that Le Play wished for: one that conformed to the social doctrines of the Catholic Church.

Accordingly, the methodological principles used to define the family monograph were challenged by Le Play's students themselves. Two of them, Edmond Demolins and Father Henri de Tourville, proposed to review and modify them where needed. To begin with, they felt the working-class family was too special an object or case. More precisely, the monograph that was designed to highlight the family's typical nature turned out actually to be a rather flat sociological study, replete with all sorts of biases. Detailing family budgets to achieve a systematic approach, as Le Play had recommended, did nothing to eradicate such biases.

Following this criticism of Le Play's family monographs, Tourville did his utmost to create a "nomenclature of social facts." In it, social facts related to the working-class family were systematically divided into 25 major classes. These classes were then subdivided into as many subheadings as there were different traits or types of a social fact. Each such fact corresponded to a set of problems ranging from the simple to the complex. Table 1.1 gives a good idea of how this inventory of social facts worked.

The nomenclature of social facts, as presented in this chart, shows the family as the node for those social facts originating in the family structure itself. Moreover, it provides a standard framework in which the systematic and comparative approach to which Tourville's family monograph aspired could be applied. Although Demolins was Tourville's ally in criticizing Le Play, he was quick to criticize Tourville for the difficulty involved in determining which types of bonds united the social facts on which his nomenclature was based. If one social fact is contained within another, causal relationships are obviously implied. The nomenclature of social facts is unable to establish such causality systematically, however.

Just as Le Play's principles and methods were questioned by his own followers, so was the very object of his monographic approach, the working-

Table 1.1   The Main Divisions of the Nomenclature

1. Means of existence		I.	Place of the family (geography and ecology)
		II.	Work of the family
		III.	Property of the family
		IV.	Movable property
		V.	Salary and wages
		VI.	Savings
2. Continuity of the race		VII.	Type of family
3. Material needs		VIII.	Standard of living and material existence of the family
		IX.	Phases of family existence
		X.	Patronage
		XI.	Commerce
4. Moral and intellectual needs		XII.	Intellectual culture
		XIII.	Religion
	a. Private sphere	XIV.	Neighborhood
		XV.	Corporations
		XVI.	County
		XVII.	Groups of counties
5. General social facts	b. Public sphere	XVIII.	The city
		XIX.	Provincial divisions
		XX.	The provinces
		XXI.	The state
	c. Foreign relations	XXII.	The expansion of the race
		XXIII.	Foreign countries
6. History of the race		XXIV.	History of the race
7. Conclusion		XXV.	Rank of the race

local { XIV–XVII }   national { XVIII–XXI }

SOURCE: Bodard-Silver (1982, p. 120). Reprinted with permission.

11

class family. Émile Cheysson was one of his first students, and an initial adherent of the family monograph. However, he began to question the pertinence of the working-class family as a key indicator of the condition of society. Social transformations sweeping across France, such as the ever-widening chasm between labor and the concentration of wealth, led him to believe that "the household is no longer the sole centre of our activity. Some of its basic attributes have been assumed by the workplace [that is, business]" (1887, p. 545).

> Thus it is clear that should an observer's studies be confined to the working class family household, only an indirect grasp will be acquired of the many phenomena which have reassembled in the workplace, along with the worker. . . . You will take a great deal of pointless trouble to go into the worker's house, and analyze his life down to the slightest details of his budget. This approach will only yield an indirect and confused glimpse of the great issues: protectionism, free trade, banks, insurance, prices, markets and competition, which nonetheless rightfully deserve to be a major public concern and to take an increasingly important role in our contemporary societies.
>
> If we want to perceive these phenomena . . ., they must be observed in the field to which they have migrated—and in which they shall henceforth prosper—the workplace. (Cheysson, 1887, p. 545)

In other words, the changes that have occurred in our society have diminished the significance of the working-class family as an observation post. Additionally, the selection of a social unit or a case that would provide for a monographic study of a society requires a clear explanation of why such a social unit would be the best place to understand the society as a whole. Le Play's method remains mute on this point. It thus suggests that the family alone is the perfect indicator of society's existence, regardless of the circumstances. This makes Le Play's method valid solely for the monograph of the working-class family and its living conditions.

Le Play's influence had waned by the turn of the century in France. Nonetheless, he continued to maintain followers outside of his country. Family monographs were produced in England by Patrick Geddes (a Scottish biologist, 1854-1932), Victor Branford (a railway engineer, 1864-1930), and A. J. Herbertson (professor of geography at Oxford University). Le Play's method also had considerable impact in Spain, Turkey, Portugal, and Hungary. In America, the method and theory of social change it implied had various degrees of influence among various American sociologists, such as Sorokin, Zimmerman, and Frampton, although they never became faithful adherents of it. Le Play's key North American follower was, in fact, a Canadian sociologist—the first French-speaking Canadian sociologist, Léon Gérin.

The monographs of the rural French-Canadian family that he published from 1905 to 1914 revived Le Play's key idea that a society could be studied on the basis of an appropriately selected social unit. Jean-Charles Falardeau, a commentator of Gérin, wrote that the latter "focused his interest on the rural family, because he saw it as the microcosm from which certain basic information on society as a whole could be inferred" (Falardeau, 1968, p. 19). But Gérin, like others who pursued Le Play's method, be they European or American, had to confront not only criticisms of it, but the opposition to the theory of social change it posited, as well. Le Play associated such social change with a reform of society corresponding to Catholic social doctrine. Le Play's theory and method embraced a conservative, even reactionary, position, and were thus highly suspect; they were widely discredited, and therefore conveniently "forgotten."

The monographic approach, and more particularly, the case study, thus disappeared from French sociology. At the most it represented a methodological interest as a yet-to-be-corroborated exploratory study. Le Play's school has recently been rediscovered, however, and this rediscovery comes during a wide-ranging debate on the possibility of approaching society as whole on the basis of a social unit strategically selected methodologically, be this a "life" (Bertaux, 1981) or a "case" on which an in-depth study could be based.

THE CHICAGO SCHOOL AND THE CASE STUDY

This debate is also present in American sociology. Le Play's school had little influence on sociology in the United States. However, American sociology was substantially influenced, at least in the beginning, by case studies produced by the Chicago School. This was the first important forum for qualitative methodology in sociology. The Chicago School requires no historical introduction (Bulmer, 1984, 1985). A very brief review will be provided here, though, on case studies undertaken by its members and the debates these studies provoked.

The case study was the approach of choice for early sociological studies in the United States, conducted by social workers and the first American sociologists, at the end of the 19th and the beginning of the 20th centuries. These initial studies concerned small, local communities and urban neighborhoods where rural and immigrant populations had recently settled. The introduction of these groups into new life settings triggered serious problems involving unemployment, poverty, delinquency, and violence.

At the turn of the century, the city of Chicago was fraught with such problems, which were aggravated by huge waves of immigration accompanied by swift urban growth. These issues were of particular interest to social workers, although they were little inclined to deal with them directly, in the field. They examined these topics chiefly through official statistics provided by health services, as well as by secondhand documents of all kinds, including various legal documents. The analysis of such materials, however, was rarely brought face-to-face with the spectacle of misery and violence apparent at that time. Through the initiative of William I. Thomas, soon aided by Robert Park, a program of field studies was set up in 1916 by the Department of Sociology at the University of Chicago, which was founded in 1892. These studies quickly triggered a whole series of case studies on problems such as poverty, delinquency, and deviance. The journalistic training of Robert Parks, who was then 50 years old, certainly inspired the method applied to these field studies. He believed that such studies demonstrated a meticulousness and a systematic approach that was lacking in journalistic accounts.

Still, the journalistic process remained. Accordingly, Parks strongly encouraged his students to go beyond official documents and come into personal contact with poverty and deviance, with notebook and city map in hand. He also recommended collecting remarks in context using open-ended interviews and a wide variety of materials, including newspaper articles and personal documents, such as letters. In so doing, Park evoked the principles employed by William Isaac Thomas, whose association with Florian Znaniecki would yield a survey of Polish immigrants, *The Polish Peasants* (1918-1920), which became a classic. It was specifically based on letters exchanged by Polish immigrants to America with family and friends who had stayed behind. The letters reveal how these people perceived their progress in the land of exile, the obstacles they encountered there, and their retrospective view of the life they left behind in their homeland.

The University of Chicago soon became a leader of the case study approach in the United States. It was a "school" in the sense that harmony prevailed between the theoretical and methodological positions of those in the Department of Sociology. The department included such luminaries as Ernest W. Burgess, Herbert Blumer, Louis Wirth, Robert Redfield, and Everett C. Hughes, all of whom had been heavily influenced by the social psychology of George H. Mead. Various personal and intellectual affiliations existed among all of them. Not so long before, Everett C. Hughes, Louis Wirth, Robert Redfield, and Herbert Blumer had all been in the same class of the first Department of Anthropology and Sociology at the University of Chicago. They had all been students of Robert Park, professor in the department since 1916, as well as of G. H. Mead. When Mead died, Hughes inherited his chair. He was to assume responsibility for publishing the complete works of Robert Park, shortly after the latter's death. Robert Redfield was the son-in-law of Robert Park, and held him in great esteem. He adopted the principles Park used in his field studies. Park's principles took inspiration from the biographic surveys of Thomas and Znaniecki, to whom Redfield had been exposed through the teachings of Ernest Burgess. Thus there existed an undeniable community of common interests and relationships that made the University of Chicago a school, although the term itself did not appear until 1940. Before that date, its members and their successors, both close and distant, would speak of the Chicago "style" or "tradition."

This community of interests was expressed first and foremost through the primary object involved in the case studies conducted there, the social problems provoked by urbanization and immigration. Within such a framework, the city is considered to be a veritable laboratory (see Grafmeyer & Joseph, 1979) providing a miniature replica of problems frequently encountered within the society. In the view of adherents of this school, the form the city takes affects these problems, in the sense that it produces them, while remaining part of them. This position also gives rise to a theoretical perspective known as *urban ecology*. Social evolution, related to the transformation of a small and simple community to a large city with its highly complex social structure, was to be explained by the ways in which any human community integrates the effects of urbanization and industrialization, using the ecological resources at their disposal. Such resources can include those afforded by the natural environment, ethnic cultures, dissemination of outside innovations, and so on.

Case studies were aimed at achieving some understanding of how these ecological resources were integrated. Such integration could be on the scale of a small community on the road to urbanization. It could also appear in a neighborhood of a city already beset by the problems urbanization

brings and which require remedies that could be provided by the ecological resources of such urban environments. These case studies were inspired methodologically by the writings of George H. Mead. These writings had, in turn, been influenced by Dewey's pragmatist philosophy. According to Dewey, social life, defined as a process or a movement, could only be understood if the meanings assigned to it by its own actors were incorporated within it. Jean Poupart wrote that "within this framework, a real knowledge of social realities requires an exploration of the personal experiences of individuals" (Poupart, Rains, & Pirès, 1983, p. 67). Such real-life or immediate experiences of social actors are explored in different ways, depending on whether a sociological study or an investigation by social service workers was involved, as was the situation in the city of Chicago. Hughes drew a clean line between these two processes in his first case studies. Sociological studies of deviance or violence, for example, could not, in his view, be reduced to relationships offering assistance, or even compassion. They must serve to explain these problems as a process pertaining to a given society. In other words, it must explain these problems as part and parcel of the life of that society.

The field study is certainly the favored approach in this area. On-site observations, open-ended interviews, and the collection of various documents are the means of choice for accomplishing this goal. Although Hughes preferred direct observation, this was not, as with Robert Park, because of a journalistic background. Rather, it was because of his familiarity with participant observation in anthropology, on which Malinowski's first studies were based. Hughes was in agreement with the principles involved in the fieldwork approach, which were designed to highlight the characteristic traits of the culture or social life under investigation. From the outset, these principles involved direct field contacts and a consideration of the meanings social actors gave their own direct experiences. Such principles are quite compatible with the system of analytic induction advocated by Thomas and Znaniecki, two leading figures from the Chicago School. In analytic induction, key working hypotheses for case studies could be developed, step by step, then validated using empirical materials collected in the field.

The case study takes shape as part of an inductive approach. In this approach, the empirical details that constitute the object under study are considered in the light of the remarks made in context. This gives depth and dimension to the sociological explanation produced by this study. The object under sociological investigation is more than mere facts or items. It is, first and foremost, an experience containing the meanings and symbols involved in the interactions of the social actors. These meanings and symbols enter into the actors' interactions, and define their points of view on these interactions. The sociological study, within the context of the symbolic interactionism favored by George H. Mead, and, particularly, the case study, must thus consider the perspective of the social actors. This will provide an understanding of the personal experiences of these actors. This direct experience is what constitutes the object under study. This position, which had been intensively developed by the Department of Sociology at the University of Chicago since 1920, has been quite clearly expressed by Howard Becker, an adherent of the Chicago School:

> To understand an individual's behaviour, we must know how he perceives the situation, the obstacles he believed he had to face, the alternatives he saw opening up to him. We cannot understand the effects of the range of possibilities, delinquent subcultures, social norms and other explanations of behaviour which are commonly invoked, unless we consider them from the actor's point of view. (Becker, 1970a, p. 64)

The actor's point of view should be given due weight, because the latter is directly present among the field materials, be they collections of remarks in context, or documents, such as letters. The case study, as we have seen thus far, is compiled from such materials. It is done so in such a way that the actors' points of view are incorporated within the sociological survey of the subject under investigation. How are the field materials that capture this point of view then constructed into sociological theory? In other words, in what ways and to what extent is the case study based on this point of view? What status does it assign it? Is the treatment of this point of view during this process of transformation defined as part of a rigorous objective process that does not solely result from the social, intellectual, and psychological makeup of the researcher? The case study approach does ensure this process of transformation. However, when all is said and done, this process was very poorly explained in the case studies of the Chicago School. It appeared to be based on theoretical tinkering, which soon caused much dissension. This was to result in the conflict over methods that even today rocks sociology and the social sciences in general. The Chicago School was at its heart, although the issues at stake go beyond this school, all the way to the basic principles of sociological study. The value of the case study was nevertheless challenged, along with the prestige that the Chicago School had enjoyed since the beginning of the century.

2. CONFLICT OF METHODS

There were no doubts about the preeminence of the Chicago School in American sociology until 1935. The case study was certainly the top-ranking method in this field, but the Chicago School was not opposed to statistical surveys. Both approaches were favored as being either complementary or exclusive, but rarely as competitive. Case studies sometimes cite statistical methods, but are still considered to be field investigations. The Chicago School dominated the networks of institutions and university media. It proudly proclaimed its leading role at meetings of the American Sociological Society, in the *American Journal of Sociology* (America's foremost sociology journal), and to financial backers. The Chicago School was the leader in intellectual life and activity in the field of sociology, and the case study consequently appeared as the methodological tool of choice in this discipline.

Still, the statistical survey gained ground in sociology, principally at Columbia University in New York, under the impetus of Franklin H. Giddings and his students, including William Ogburn. Giddings and his students formed the "F.H.G. Club . . . characterized by its anti-Chicago sentiments and a marked preference for statistical methods over case studies" (Pirès, 1982, p. 19). Rivalry quickly developed between this institution and the Chicago School. The key issue focused primarily, but not exclusively, on methodology. In other words, although statistical methods were well accepted as part of the case study, they were considered no more than tools useful for surveying the object under study. The development of these methods at Columbia would result is a wide variety of techniques, intended not only to provide explanations but also to serve as a basis for forecasts.

Disputes over the relevance of the case study were rife not only at Columbia, but, rather curiously, within the Chicago School itself. In 1927, Ogburn, a student of Giddings, and a steadfast adherent of statistical methods, was hired by Chicago to teach graduate sociology students about the utility of statistical methods. He clearly described the virtues of such methods and placed special emphasis on their capacity to validate a theoretical idea, just as in the experimental sciences. Without such a capacity, sociology could not claim to be a science. The lecture he gave in 1930 as president of the American Sociological Society openly stated this preference. In Ogburn's view if an

> idea of value to science must be formulated in some sort of form capable of demonstration or proof . . . verification in this future state of scientific sociology will amount almost to a fetish. . . . It must always be remembered that science grows by accretion, by the accumulation of little bits and pieces of new knowledge. [This means] . . . that all sociologists [must] be statisticians. (quoted by Bryant, 1985, p. 137)

Validation of sociological theories requires researchers to hold any subjective attitudes or feelings they may have in check while carrying out their studies.

> It will be necessary to crush out emotion and to discipline the mind so strongly that the fanciful pleasures of intellectuality will have to be eschewed in the verification process: it will be desirable to taboo ethics and values (except in choosing problems); and it will be inevitable that we shall have to spend most of our time doing hard, dull, tedious, and routine tasks. (Ogburn, quoted in Bryant, 1985, p. 138)

Ogburn's comments were to be echoed in the dissertation of one of his students, Samuel Stouffer, which was published in condensed form as an article (Stouffer, 1931). He showed that statistical methods can yield results quite close to those of case studies, but could do so more economically and expeditiously. Furthermore, they could comply with validation requirements then appearing in American sociology, including the Chicago School. This preference for validation would rapidly give rise to a new method of study in sociology. This would be one that would support sociology's claim to be a fully controlled form of analysis, a science.

To begin with, the new method required a theoretical basis, or foundation, aimed at explaining a given social issue. Testing this theory involved a deductive process incorporating technical procedures that could demonstrate its accuracy, while eliminating any bias on the part of the researcher or the empirical context. This method also ruled out any direct contact between the researcher and the empirical context, the very contact required by the participant-observation method, which was deemed to lack rigor and to be subject to personal impressions. In other words, the statistical method considered field data to be secondary or trivial and drew a very clear distinction between such data and sociological theory.

Without actually going into the history of American sociology, it would be appropriate to note that this demarcation heralded the institutionalization of sociology and the refinement of its first general theories, primarily due to Talcott Parsons. Theoretical work in sociology thereby acquired a predominant role, thus breaking with field studies, which had, until that time, been associated with "commonplace evidence," likely to lead sociology explanations astray from the kind of rigor that should inspire the discipline. The value of this explanation thus relies on theoretically defined rules and tools. To a certain extent these tools involve a departure from common sense, that is, with the meanings social actors assign to their own experiences. Such common sense is, and must be, considered suspect in producing sociological theories, because it draws on empirical elements, false truths that compromise its value and its rigor.

The case study has obviously been the target of much criticism on this basis, as common sense, the universe of meanings intrinsic to the personal experience of the social actors, constitutes the empirical foundations of the sociological theory aimed at explaining it. It is thus difficult to validate such a theory, because it is based on meanings that fall outside the requirements of the theoretical process itself. Case studies were also rejected because of the lack of assurance that any sociological explanation or theory spawned by them would be sufficiently general. In other words, how could one particular case explain a problem in general terms? Even more important, how could such generality be achieved in the absence of evidence that the case study is truly representative?

The conflict that openly pitted the members of the Chicago School against the faculty of New York's Columbia University was based precisely on these points, issues concerning the definition of the sociological investigation from the perspective of existing methods. It would, however, quickly degenerate into a political brawl between these two institutions over the control of financial resources and media that could enable either to achieve a hegemony over the other, ensuring that its methodological principles would triumph.

The dispute became public at the 1935 annual meeting of the American Sociological Society,[1] during which the strong hold of the Chicago School over this association, its meetings, and its publication, the *American Journal of Sociology*, was sharply repudiated. Columbia University faculty sought to avoid Chicago's control by creating a new journal, the

American Sociological Review, as well as networks of collaboration in which statistical methods were held in esteem. The control of the Chicago School was strongly decried and, in the heat of this opposition, the case study was reexamined to the point of being rejected, not just because of its weak points, but more important, due to its exclusive relationship with this school. Methodological critiques of the case study were often no more than political arguments intended to undermine the Chicago School's dominance among American universities.

This dominance would soon erode, and the case study elicited increasingly less interest. From this point on, statistical methods would be required in all sociological studies. The introduction of these methods seemed to make it possible for such studies to become controlled experiments, like lab tests in the experimental sciences. Oddly enough, the principles involved in similar methods were tacitly confirmed by Chicago School adherents. The result was that strict guidelines for the case study were defined by its own defenders.

The case study thus became an exploratory investigation, a preliminary survey giving rise to a statistical study that could validate or eliminate a theory or a general model. Although not too long before the case study had been a sociological study in and of itself, it was about to become a point of departure to be consolidated within an established theory that could validate its general applicability. The result was a reversal in the process by which field materials were constructed into sociological theory. In the Chicago School tradition, theory was built from field materials. In the statistical method, theory gave dimension to, and even validated, the representativeness of empirical data. This reversal was undoubtedly tied to the appearance in the 1930s of the first general theories in American sociology. These were principally produced by Talcott Parsons. His methods for testing them were, to a certain extent, devoted to the scientific virtues of this discipline. The claims resulting from this point of view tended to make sociology abstract, detached from its empirical context, and quite unwilling to base any statistical models on such a context. Paul Lazarsfeld, an eminent advocate of the statistical studies conducted at Columbia, would go so far as to say that "he could spend hours playing with mathematical models . . . [that] data in itself held little interest for him . . . [and that, as for the rest] the value lies in manipulating them with statistical tools" (Champagne, 1982, p. 5). The emphasis was thus placed on the ability of these models to validate theories in order to prove their generality.

The case study lacked such virtues. Built on a single case, it can with difficulty measure a theory's generality, except in assuming other cases to be similar. Case study adherents, including those of the Chicago School, began assessing case studies in terms of the standards of verification applicable to statistical methods. Under such circumstances, the case study gradually came to be seen "in the best case, as a pre-scientific heuristic study, and no longer as an inherently valid form of knowledge, as it had previously been considered in Chicago" (Pirès, 1982, p. 17).

The case study had its heyday in American sociology with the Chicago School. The methodological conflict that erupted between adherents of this school and those of statistical methods resulted in a decline of interest in the case study, beginning in the early 1940s. The dispute over this issue, as well as over qualitative methods in general, seemed to be inspired by a rigorous approach, which, presumably, would be better assured through the implementation of statistical methods. Although the conflict of methods was linked to this issue, it was contested on a strictly political playing field. The key issue was the hegemony that Columbia University and the Chicago School wished to exert within the American university community. It would be difficult, in such a setting, to determine if criticisms of the case study were dictated by methodological considerations, or if they had more to do with struggles between university institutions. The stakes involved in the struggle were obviously of a much different nature (Bulmer, 1984; Pirès, 1982).

Whatever the situation, it is quite interesting to reassess the criticisms of the Chicago School's case study approach in the light of studies that provide an excellent illustration of it and that were conducted by some of its leading figures. Two works are of particular significance in this regard. The first is *Saint-Denis, a French-Canadian Parish*, by Horace Miner (1939), and the second is *French Canada in Transition*, by Everett C. Hughes (1943). As their titles indicate, they deal with French-Canadian (or what is now known as Quebec) society, rather than that of the United States. Because Quebec society is easily distinguished from American society, along with the industrialization and urbanization that characterize the latter, it is of sociological interest. Miner's work concerned French-Canadian culture. His aim was to delineate its key features, using the case of the village of Saint-Denis de Kamouraska. Hughes's work is intended to deal with the influence of ethnicity on the division of labor within a small, primarily Francophone town. This town, Drummondville (called "Cantonville" in Hughes's work), was undergoing profound social changes, in the aftermath of an influx of capital controlled by Anglophones. Our object is not to discuss the results of Miner's and Hughes's studies in detail but rather to consider the relevance of criticisms made of the methodology of the case study.

The case study has basically been faulted for:

1. its lack of representativeness, and especially the lack of representativeness of the case used as a point of observation for the social phenomenon or issue constituting the object of study; and

2. its lack of rigor in the collection, construction, and analysis of the empirical materials that give rise to this study. This lack of rigor is linked to the problem of bias. Such bias is introduced by the subjectivity of the researcher, as well as of the field informants on whom the researcher relies to get an understanding of the case under investigation.

These two points synopsize the criticisms made of the case study. More broadly, however, they are also the most conspicuous problems in any sociological study.

At first glance, the lack of representativeness would seem to characterize the case study as Miner and Hughes conceived of it, for example. This is because they used one particular case, or a single observation point, to study a social issue or phenomenon. The selection of this point of observation is the first problem. We might look at what considerations go into determining it. How could the selection of a village like Saint-Denis de Kamouraska, in the case of Miner, or a small town like Drummondville, for Hughes, represent the French Canada of that era as a whole? Was this, perhaps, due to some picturesque impression people entertained of French Canada? Or, was it to sanctify America's hold over the economic and social development of Quebec or French Canada? To view French-Canadian society as a traditional one, underdeveloped within the prevailing North American context, served, in a certain sense, to justify the American presence and ensure its transformation. Thus, undertaking such studies "is a key part of the dialectical process dignifying the colonizer, and humiliating the colonized" (Sales, 1979, p. 147).

In other words, it is not certain that the cases on which these studies had been based were representative. Yet, what is it that these cases might have failed to represent? Critiques of the representativeness of Chicago School case studies do not discuss the reasons why these sociologists conducted their studies in Quebec (French Canada). However, Miner is quite clear on this point in the introduction to his work:

> The study reported in this volume set out to give an ethnographic description of the rural French-Canadian folk culture in its least-altered existent form. . . . To satisfy the requirements of the study, a long-established agricultural community was sought which had maintained the old culture to a large degree. St. Denis admirably suited these requirements. Other parishes in Quebec which are more physically isolated are more recently settled or are dependent upon a diversified economy. Many more have become towns and cities. St. Denis was selected as possessing none of these drawbacks. (Miner, 1939, p. ix)

The selection of Saint-Denis de Kamouraska was thus not an arbitrary one, considering that the very object of Horace Miner's study was the traditional French-Canadian culture he hoped to understand. The village proved to be an excellent vantage point for studying this traditional rural culture. This village was thus selected on the basis of a real methodological strategy aimed at coming into contact with this rural culture "in its least altered form," in a society whose culture had changed elsewhere. Miner recognized that there had been changes in rural French-Canadian culture, but that was not the object of his study, and this was also what made Saint-Denis de Kamouraska so valuable.

Thus the representative value of cases selected in the case study method has been critically perceived. No doubt this is because representativeness has been too closely linked to ethnographic studies. The main goal of the latter is to "map institutions or speech forms, corpuses listing types of traditional dwellings or themes in folk tales . . . which gather together by region the beliefs and rituals which traditionally mark the various ages of life or the calendar of feast days" (Zonabend, 1992, pp. 49-50). In other words, this is an ethnography aimed at examining folklore and customs. In and of itself, it defines a very specific object of study. In the words of French anthropologist Françoise Zonabend: "This is how macroscopic research became microscopic, and unique, singular and personal research emerged from a uniformity, giving rise to a common criticism of this approach to the effect that the groups under study lack representativeness" (1992, p. 51).

The value of representativeness, as we can see, is not so much a function of the group or case under investigation as it is of the object of study that can be approached from this point of observation chosen for the study of one particular case. Chicago School case studies have eluded such criticism about their representativeness, since this is always defined in terms of the object of study. The work of Miner clearly illustrated this principle.

Furthermore, the frequency with which the issue of the lack of rigor in the case study has been raised would suggest a total absence of objectivity. This absence would primarily result from the intrusion of subjectivity, from field informants used to collect firsthand information, as well as from the researcher, whose research is based on personal observations. Such observations presumably involve the latter's participation. This approach is subjective in that the ideas, thoughts, representations, and values of the informants and researcher stand in the way of an exact reconstruction of elements that could define the phenomenon, the object of study.

Without immediately engaging in a discussion of the often-debated concept of objectivity in sociology, and, more generally, in the social sciences, we should closely examine the process involved in producing a case study. Hughes's (1943) case study, *French Canada in Transition*, clearly illustrates this process.

His study of the consequences of industrialization on the small French-Canadian town of Drummondville in 1933 is based on official statistics, examinations of archives and newspapers, testimonials collected by himself and his wife, as well as on personal observations of the daily life within the community undergoing profound change. Secondhand materials, such as official statistics, items from archives, and news clippings, provide an initial overview of such transformations. These materials are like pieces in a puzzle that is assembled based on the impact of ethnicity on the division of labor within a community undergoing changes triggered by industrialization financed by foreign capital. The makeup of the puzzle serves as a "backdrop" (this is the title of the first part of Hughes's work). In a certain way, it provides a portrait of the situation as revealed in the official registers of political, civic, religious, academic, and other institutions. Information contained in such registers has already been structured according to the needs of such institutions. Hughes thus merely draws on a portion of it, in some cases. In others, selected information has been accentuated by theories obtained from other sociological studies, such as those of Gérin and Miner, as well as work in political science, demography, and geography. This demonstrates how well Hughes's study of sociology fits in with other social sciences, such as human geography, demography, and political science. The interdisciplinary application of these other methods enables him to provide a multifaceted view of his own subject.

Which theoretical perspectives are to be included is thus essentially determined by the object under investigation. In this case, the ethnic nature of the division of labor is linked to the impact of foreign industrialization in a community with a homogeneous culture, and for this reason does not call into play a theoretical patchwork with no clearly stated focus.

The inclusion of these various theoretical perspectives enabled Hughes to distance himself initially from information that, although already organized by the needs of the institutions that collected it, still served to form the backdrop for his own sociological study. Comments directly collected from field informants, along with observations taken directly from daily life, further enabled Hughes to remain aloof from officially collected information, as well as hypotheses formed to explain both this information and that yielded by fieldwork.

Such detachment is primarily ensured by constant confrontation within the framework of the case study. If the subjectivity of the researcher and of field informants is presented within this study, it is entirely possible to clearly distinguish them by comparison. Chapoulie's (1986-1987) study of Hughes's work raises this point in great detail:

> But the comparative method not only permits field researchers to take an objective point of view toward their own activities and thus exercise a certain control over them, it also allows them to avoid established representations of the subjects they study, especially those associated with their own familiar everyday points of view. (p. 276)
>
> Hughes thus used the comparative method, not for demonstrating proofs, but to construct analytic categories free from value judgements and from the categories used by workers themselves (or by their employers) for practical purposes. (p. 278)

It is undoubtedly unnecessary to cite the comparative method to characterize Hughes's approach, as Chapoulie does here. Because they can be compared directly, it is possible to note aspects ensuing from the subjectivity of the field informants and to see where the researcher's own subjectivity enters in. The contrast shown by this comparison provides an understanding of the object of study as defined by the comments of field informants, and as constructed by the researcher to explain the object from a sociological perspective. The impact of the subjectivity of field informants, as well as that of the researcher, are clearly distinguished in this manner. Moreover, such a distinction is clearly expressed in the case study.

Criticisms of the case study concerning its presumed lack of representativeness and methodological rigor appear poorly founded, at least if the work of Miner and Hughes is considered characteristic of the Chicago

School. Such criticism was made in the heat of a methodological conflict in sociology fueled more by issues dealing with the relative importance of university institutions than by the virtues of the methods being disputed. The case study is not without its drawbacks. They are related to the state of development of sociology and the sociological method at the time when this methodological conflict broke out, announcing the case study's final hours of glory.

Subsequent advances in quantitative methods undoubtedly marked the swift decline of the case study in sociology, as well as in most other social sciences, except for anthropology, where it has remained popular. Although these advances have also permitted undeniable progress in sociological methodology, the limits of qualitative methods became rapidly evident in the methodological approach to sociological objects of study. Repudiated in the early 1960s with an intensity reminiscent of the virulence of the conflict of methods that was so widespread some 30 years before, the inherent problems and confines of quantitative methods have propagated renewed interest in the case study, and more generally, in qualitative methods.

This renewed interest sparked a return to the Chicago School, and even led to the formation of a new or second Chicago School (see bibliography) represented in particular by Anselm Strauss and Barney Glaser (1967), founders of *grounded theory*, as well as Howard Becker (1963). Like Strauss, the latter was a student of Hughes, whose influence may be seen in Becker's case studies of jazz musicians and marijuana smokers.

The new Chicago School is certainly not the only illustration of developments marking this renewed interest in the case study. An earlier indicator had been the "community studies" tradition as evidenced in William F. Whyte's (1981) famous study, *Street Corner Society*. The "new ethnography," highlighted by such figures as James Clifford (1980) and George E. Marcus (Clifford & Marcus, 1986), also played a role in the renewal of the case study. In France, sociological and historical perspectives were moving closer together: This exchange was especially fruitful in the discussion of methodological problems resulting from case studies, beginning with problems regarding the generalization value of any one case (Wieviorka, 1992). This book can but briefly survey these new developments, rather than analyzing them in detail. Only some of the considerations arising from them are therefore presented in the following chapter. The bibliography at the end of the book can also serve as an invitation

to discover the many works examining these new developments in the case study.

Note

1. In 1958, the American Sociological Society became the American Sociological Association, notably to avoid any misunderstandings resulting from its acronym, ASS.

3. THE CURRENT DEBATE ON THE CASE STUDY

This revival of the case study and of qualitative methods in sociology provides an excellent occasion to discuss the questions and issues such methods pose in sociological research. In other words, what does this discipline attempt to explain? We shall consider at least some of these questions and issues in light of research conducted on the case study and on qualitative methodology. The scope, diversity, and background of this research is described in the accompanying bibliography.

The history of sociological methodology and, more particularly, the well-known conflict in sociological methods have clearly revealed that the methodological questions and issues involved in this discipline, cannot be appropriately considered, or for that matter resolved, by the opposition of quantitative and qualitative methods. Seen from within this perspective, sociology's methodological problems generate no more than "failed debates" (Pirès, 1982). They could have been, and were not, opportunities for the discipline to display the progress and the rigor it must demonstrate. It is, however, difficult to examine these problems without returning to and renewing the famous methodological conflict in which they were involved not so long ago. Nonetheless, this is what we shall now attempt to do.

The Problem of the Theory and of Its Validation

The stakes involved in the conflict that pitted Chicago School case study adherents against supporters of Columbia University's statistical methods resulted in the requirement that sociological study be able to validate its theories. All sociological studies must start off with a theory based on a review of the sociological literature relating to the subject under investigation. This theory must then be validated through the study of a specific object, phenomenon, or social problem. Such validation constitutes proof of its explanatory value. This requirement is drawn from the deductive method used in the experimental sciences. In this context, any science must be able to "reconstruct facts, give them meaning within the scope of a theory or theoretical framework, and, using a set of review procedures, provide analytical methods" (Godelier, 1982, p. 24).

Although this deductive approach is traditionally used to corroborate any scientific theory, whether the latter falls within the field of experimental science or a social science like sociology, a theory must be constructed before it can be validated. This may initially appear quite evident. Put in other words, a theory or theoretical framework first emerges from the study of an empirical case or object, the approach to which is not and cannot be deductively defined. History, and scientific epistemology, now clearly recognize that "there is no scientific 'method,' recipe or algorithm known that will permit scientific discovery. We know of no mechanical means that will generate a hypothesis or theory based on certain facts observed in a finite series of steps" (Jacob, 1989, p. 10). All theories are initially based on a particular case or object. The in-depth study of this case or study will elicit one or more theories that could be validated by other objects or cases. This process will assess their general applicability. Validation of a theory should not neglect the fact that its refinement has been the result of a process whose genealogy "lends itself more to a historical than to a logical approach" (p. 11). The emphasis placed on validating a theory, an issue at the very core of the methodological conflict, has undoubtedly resulted in some avoidance of this point. The proof is that theories do not appear to be based on empirical elements. Rather, they consist of a set of proposals or abstract theories. The general applicability of their explanatory value must be assessed by validating these empirical elements. Nonetheless, it is indeed "the empirical description of such elements which yields good theoretical questions. If they are based on a new factual element, as Bachelard said, they can pave the way to a discovery of the general structure of some sphere of reality" (Godelier, 1982, p. 25).

The emphasis placed on theoretical validation becomes even more stringent when it is taken to imply that the theory runs counter to empirical facts, and, even more so, to any meanings that might be assigned them. The dominant status thus assigned to theory suggests that it should radically distinguish itself from empirical facts. It should do so by running against the grain of direct experience, since the primary purpose of theory is to understand such experience in some way other than in terms of its immediacy. This factor should be even more apparent in the field of sociology and the other social sciences, because the social experience with which these disciplines is concerned is actually created from meanings provided by the social actors themselves.

THE STATUS OF FIELD MATERIALS

As a result, sociological theory must distinguish itself from the meanings social actors attribute to their own personal experiences. These meanings are considered in this context as common sense, the status of which, in the social sciences and more particularly in sociology, has been rather poorly received. Common sense has thus been defined, by degree, as commonplace evidence, malformed mirrors of reality, a false awareness, or an awareness that is incorrect (Houle, 1986). The specific point of the theory is to circumvent such commonplace evidence, to achieve an explanation that can be rigorously demonstrated. The case study is of no help in this regard, inasmuch as the empirical description of the social facts that characterize it are based on common sense.

The requirement placed on the social sciences, and particularly on sociology, to circumvent commonplace evidence, common sense, has never been so well stated as in the structuralism based on the work of French anthropologist Claude Lévi-Strauss. Maurice Godelier (1980) wrote:

> Scientific representation of social reality does not occur through the "abstraction" of the spontaneous or considered representations [or meanings] of individuals. Rather, it must dispute the evidence of these representations to display the concealed internal logic of the social reality. The refusal to accept visible social relationships as "the" social reality is also the case with Claude Lévi-Strauss. He has based his structural analysis on a rejection of any empirical assumptions. (p. 111)

It thus follows that:

> The problem with scientific knowledge is thus to determine its points of departure. These cannot be the spontaneous representations provided by individuals in their relationships—representations which they pragmatically use each day to produce and reproduce their existence within these relationships, along with such relationships themselves. Most of the time, these representations serve as the "actual evidence" for individuals acting within their relationships and on their relationships, but who are prisoners of them. (Godelier, 1980, p. 111)

Similarly, the meanings assigned directly by social actors to their own social experiences cannot serve in any form as the point of departure for theory, as these meanings of representations will not reveal "the concealed internal logic of the social reality." These direct meanings serve as a screen. Under such circumstances, theory must surpass such evidence to grasp the social reality that appears to be hidden beneath it. Lévi-Strauss risked using the term *unconsciousness* to describe the fact that the meanings assigned by social actors to their own social experiences cannot explain the properties of the social relationships that make up their direct experience. Revealing these properties requires the introduction of theoretical models, such as the logical-mathematical models that Lévi-Strauss used to reveal the structure of kinship systems, myths, table manners, and so forth. (For more on Lévi-Strauss's work, see Marc-Lipiansky, 1973.) The application of this system permitted explanation to take place on another level than that of the meanings that were actually assigned to them.

The case study has been roundly criticized for its reliance on common sense. However, no such complaints were made about the fact that the set of empirical materials from which all sociological studies proceed, include, to varying extents, meanings that social actors assign to their own social experiences. Such meanings may appear in an autobiographical account, as well as in a letter or in replies to a questionnaire, although in the last case strict controls are applied. Such control does nothing, however, to change the fact that it is the actors' meanings that appear in the answers to the questions they have been asked about their social reality; that is, the social reality of which they are an active part.

The negative status conferred on the meanings of social actors, and thus on the materials that they possess, poses problems, as all sociological studies ultimately rely on commonplace evidence or on a false awareness of social reality. How, under such circumstances, is it possible to rigorously reveal the "real" social reality, using materials whose negatively perceived contents serve as a point of departure? It would be difficult to assign such a negative status to the empirical materials from which all sociological studies proceed, and thus, to the direct meanings social actors attribute to their social experiences. Moreover, recent research on ideology and common sense tends to show that the value of meanings given by actors to their social experiences is relative to such experiences.[1] Under such circumstances, it would be difficult to confer such a negative status on them, because these meanings constitute the direct knowledge that social actors have of their experience or of their social reality.

These meanings of social actors thus are introduced from the outset into the set of empirical materials used by any sociological study, whether such materials were taken from life or not. Lévi-Strauss used the discovery of the properties of social relationships to explain social experience on a level other than the immediate one, that of the meanings assigned by social actors. This discovery refers us back to the study of such materials to reveal these properties.

THE DESCRIPTION AND THE BREAKDOWN OF SOCIAL EXPERIENCE

To begin with, empirical materials should be studied within the context of the purpose Lévi-Strauss saw in sociology, and more generally, in the social sciences. This purpose is to explain the direct experiences of social actors from the perspective of the social relationships that constitute such experiences. This first requires that direct experience, as understood through various empirical materials, be broken down into objects that could reveal the properties of the social relationships that make up these experiences. By *object of study* we mean "that which may be used to construct [theoretical] models, which can be manipulated according to explicit rules, and which can be evaluated using specifically defined and codified tests" (Granger, 1989, p. 17). This process involves consolidating collected empirical materials into an object of study that will reveal the properties involved in the social relationships that constitute the direct experiences of social actors. Such consolidation thus corresponds to the breakdown that complies with this goal. At its best, this process characterizes the sociological study. In short, such a reduction is achieved by breaking out, from among the entire set of empirical materials, all information pertinent to the social relationships that define the subject that is the focus of the sociological study.

This breakdown is complicated by the fact that the information contained in the empirical materials is established based on meanings assigned by the actors to their social realities, or preferably, to their direct experiences. Discovering the properties of these social relationships requires that the object that could reveal them be described as it is defined within the context of the direct meanings that appear in the selected empirical materials. Understanding the empirical properties of social relationships consequently requires such a description, enabling us to establish the manner in which the object of study determined according to this objective has been concretely defined, within the actual context of the experiences of the social actors and meanings they assign directly to such experiences. From the outset, the case study appears to serve this purpose. As it has been traditionally defined, it proves to be the descriptive study, par excellence and in depth. The case study thus serves as "the most complete and detailed sort of presentation of the subject under investigation," made possible "by giving special attention to totalizing in the observation, reconstruction and analysis of the objects under study" (Zonabend, 1992, p. 52). In this sense, it is the type of study best suited to understanding the way in which the subject under investigation by the researcher (sociologist or anthropologist) is defined or established within the meanings of the social actors, by the description of the object as the study develops.

Such a description is produced "in a mixture of social science language and the language of everyday life" (Chapoulie, 1986-1987, p. 272). This makes it possible to understand the way in which the researcher describes, in action and in his or her theoretical language, the object of the study that is defined directly in the language of daily life, which is the set of meanings social actors assign to their own experiences, which in turn constitute common sense. The transformation of the experience or social reality defined according to the meanings assigned directly by the social actors to the social experience as intended and determined by sociological theory is thus clarified by the description rendered by the case study, under ideal circumstances. The detail and depth of the description rendered by the case study permit an understanding of the empirical foundations of the theory. At the same time, the manner in which empirical elements are theoretically defined may also be clearly understood. Description is not, however, in and of itself, explanation. According to Lévi-Strauss, the latter always requires an application of abstract and theoretical models. Nonetheless, this description is still mandatory. It is needed to ensure that the empirical foundations on which the theory will be constructed can be precisely defined. The case study thereby attains a key importance in sociology and the other social sciences, in that it has proven to be a powerful descriptive study. Canadian epistemologist Gilles Houle's comments clearly underline this point:

> The known explanatory theories, much envied by the social sciences, were all preceded by *descriptive* theories on which they could base themselves. The Chicago School remains a key reference on this point, through the clarification it made possible of the "rules" of description. The monograph

remains the best example of this process, largely through the variety of data used. Thus, the case study considered as theory, as well as descriptive methods in general, can no longer be seen as a prehistorical stage of sociology. (Houle, 1986, p. 45)

Consequently, the case study does not go against the grain of theoretical sociological models; it permits them to exist under more propitious conditions. Viewed in this light, they take on immediate value for the actual purpose of explanation, in sociology and in the other social sciences.

Furthermore, if all explanatory theory appears in the form of a model, it is because the explanation determined through this form has general applicability and thus does not apply to any particular case. The case study is, in fact, by definition, the in-depth study of a particular case. How then could it have any explanatory, and thus general value? These questions impose a return to the same old issue of the representativeness of the case under investigation.

A Few Considerations on the Movement From Local to Global

The case study appears inadequate on these two points, because it is based on only one particular case. The scope of the study is thus only relative to that case, and, accordingly, can only be considered microscopic. From this viewpoint, the case study only permits the understanding of a single facet that is intrinsic to the case under investigation. In this way it has become the ideal tool for microsociological investigation. Studying other cases makes it possible to moderate not only the limits, but the failings, of such a microsociological study, as comparison between cases puts the first study into perspective. When all is said and done, this is the most commonly accepted position in sociology on this subject. It is even affirmed by sociologists who, like Anthony Giddens (1984b), for example, take strong exception to the famous distinction between micro- and macrosociology: "Pieces of ethnographic research like . . . the traditional small-scale community research of fieldwork anthropology—are not in themselves generalizing studies. But they can easily become such if carried out in some numbers, so that judgements of their typicality can justifiably be made" (p. 328).

The case study is thus only microscopic for want of "a sufficient number" of cases, as Giddens put it. The problem here is to determine exactly how many cases are needed. Is the scope of the case study best established on the basis of 2, 10, or 100 cases? Does this scope become macroscopic the moment a study involves more than one case?

The issue of the scope of the case study involves a review of problems and considerations previously discussed regarding the representativeness of cases investigated. This does not require repetition here. However, we have seen that, in the heat of sociology's methodological conflicts, the emphasis placed on numbers of cases considered raised the question of the suitability of any case for the purposes of a sociological investigation. This question applied whether or not such an investigation was based on a case study. It emerged that the definition of such suitability resides in the study's actual aim. What is this case (or are these cases) intended to explain? Even if the number of cases is a significant factor in the definition of any sociological investigation, it is not a paramount issue. Nor could this issue, in and of itself, serve to define such an investigation. In other words, although the number of studies conducted is important, no sociological investigation can be defined on the basis of that issue alone.

Because the objectives of a sociological investigation can help determine what number of cases are required, it would appear that such an investigation could be constructed from a single case, as long as the latter proves adequate to meet this objective. In Pierre Bourdieu's recently published discussions with his student, Loïc Wacquant, he appropriately noted that "there was no need for Galileo to constantly repeat the slope experiment to construct the falling body model. A well-constructed single case is no longer singular" (Bourdieu, 1992, p. 57). The methodological virtues or qualities of a selected case make it "a well-constructed single case." The esteemed anthropologist Clifford Geertz neatly synopsized this point in his remarks on the methodological virtues of the village, formerly considered the anthropologist's territory of choice:

> The best type of village structure [for anthropologists] might be formulated by representing it using the model in which theoretically distinct plans of social organization intersect. . . . A village is neither a hamlet nor a group attending the same church. It is a concrete example of the intersection of different levels of social organization within a broadly defined location. (Geertz, 1959, quoted in Champagne, 1982, p. 11)

The village, as it was methodologically perceived, at least in the days of the first anthropologists,[2] proved to be an excellent observation point for understanding different types of social organization. The most salient

features and properties of such social organizations were revealed where
the different types intersected. As Lévi-Strauss put it, an explanation of
the properties of social relationships can thus be produced through the
study of a single case, for example, a village. Such a study would produce
a macro- rather than a microsociological explanation. The methodological
qualities of the case thereby determine its representative value, in line
with the aim of the study. The case's representative value is further
clarified by its description in the case study. On this subject, anthropologist Zonabend (1992) said:

> Only the monographic approach . . . makes it possible to determine the
> sociologically relevant conditions of representativeness since, while describ-
> ing the concrete processes leading to the formation of social customs or the
> evolution of institutions, it reveals the most important factors and the most
> crucial points of rupture, at least for those [cases] under investigation. (p. 51)

The representativeness noted here is sociological in nature. In other
words, it has been constructed within an initial sociological theory applying to the case under investigation, a theory whose formulation is made
up of a holistic description of the case. The degree of detail in the description of the case study thus serves to ensure that the representativeness of
the case under investigation has been defined in a manner that is clearly
apparent. This will then make it possible to grasp directly, in action, we
might say, how the case under investigation is representative of the society
that is the subject of the explanation. Representativeness is thereby
ensured by the "sociological imagination" displayed in the methodological tactics and selections employed in determining which case should be
used, or more accurately, which subject should be investigated. The scope
of the case study is based on such choices and tactics, the methodological
qualities of which may be understood in action, through the description
provided of the object under study.

The movement from local to global is determined by identifying singularities and understood in the sense used in mathematics and scientific
epistemology. This would be the position that René Thom (1975, 1983)
neatly describes, as introduced in his "catastrophe theory." The following
extract from an interview with this famous mathematician summarizes
simply a position based on epistemological reasoning, which cannot be
presented in detail here:

Jean Petitot: What relationship do you see between element/aggregate opposition and local/global opposition? How is the concept of singularity crucial in this respect?

René Thom: The concept of singularity is important for a very basic reason. It is one of two tools a mathematician can use to go from the local to the global. Any deduction, in fact, requires a move from local to global. These two tools go in the opposite direction. The first, which goes from the local to the global, is that of analytical extension. We must recognize that all existing methods of quantitative prediction are ultimately based on it. The second tool, which goes from the global to the local, is specifically that of singularities. In a singularity, a global being is concentrated within a point. It can be reconstructed through deployment or desingularization.

Jean Petitot: This is a reversal of semantic connotations. Singularity has become the correct object, after having traditionally been the incorrect one. Thus you believe that singularities structure phenomena?

René Thom: Yes. I believe that singularities are the skeletons of phenomena. (Petitot, 1977, p. 31)

If these selections and tactics determine that the object studied is representative of the selected society, the scope of the study thus proves to be macroscopic through the methodological virtues that these selections and tactics display. The definition of its sociological representativeness confers a scope to the selected case or subject, so that an in-depth study of it will yield explanations of the properties inherent in social relationships, and thus, that which predominates on a global scale in society. The case under investigation, through the methodological qualities assigned to it pursuant to the explanation of the recommended tactics and selections, becomes a sort of experimental prototype, to make an analogy with laboratory tests in the exact or natural sciences.

In other words, what is an experimental prototype in these fields if not a device, instruments, or machines whose theoretical, methodological, or even technical definitions of their uses represent the living or inanimate material that constitutes the object of study? Matter is thus represented in miniature through this experimental prototype in the sense that, through its definition, and based on methodological and theoretical tactics and selections, it is globally reproduced on this scale. Such an experimental prototype, for example, condenses living matter, nature, and places to an extremely local and reduced scale. This permits an understanding of it and an explanation of its properties, which, on such a scale, become evident.

In accordance with this definition, an experimental prototype makes it possible to perceive the singularity of the object of study, and in so doing, ensures the transformation from local to global necessary for its explanation.

Singularity is thus characterized as a concentration of the global in the local. Singularity is not perceived as a particular feature of a fact, a species, or a thing. It is seen, rather, as characterizing a fact, a species, or a thing. It is clearly in this respect that the position of well-known mathematician Thom serves to reverse the semantic connotation previously suggested by Petitot. Science epistemologist Gilles-Gaston Granger echoes Thom in his belief that the method involved in discovering singularities and in making the transformation from the local to the global may be summarized in three words: describing, understanding, and explaining.

> "Describing something well requires an understanding of it," wrote Thom. Better yet, we might add, such a description should attempt to explain. By "explain," we mean the relationship of the *local* to the *global*, which this mathematician so aptly emphasized. We have already seen that he describes singularity as a "concentration" of the global in the local. But, he more generally suggests that the theoretical method is opposed to the pragmatic one in the same way as the scope of global problems—to be resolved by reduction to typical local situations—is opposed to the scope of local problems—which are to be resolved through global means. . . . He recognized the existence of this dual orientation within science itself. But [theory] as he perceives it, would essentially presume the movement involved in the dominance of qualitative knowledge, and which uses singularities to detect the global within them and thereby reconstruct them. (Granger, 1988, pp. 116-117)

We should briefly return to the three words associated with a method, which, according to Granger (1988), is that of qualitative scientific knowledge, in the best sense of the word. Description should be understood to be the illustration of a whole and its sectioning into parts. "The instrument of this referencing operation is a canvas, or abstract network, appropriately suited to the placement of fragments of the puzzle and the reconstruction of the whole through its parts" (pp. 117-118).

> "Understanding" certainly presumes that a sufficiently adequate and precise description already exists—however brief it might be. But we can only understand the form if we establish the relationships and forces that link the parts in which the description has sectioned the whole. A purely descriptive

sectioning could easily be entirely arbitrary; a comprehensive sectioning requires relationships to emerge between the "fragments." (Granger, 1988, pp. 117-118)

Thus, explaining means "inserting this system into a broader one on which its genesis, stability and decline will ultimately depend" (Granger, 1988, pp. 117-118). The result is that relationships and forces that link the parts in the form of the whole will themselves be understood within their singularity, in its previously discussed sense. Each part, like all of the rest, can then be understood within the process of transformation from the local to the global, since the singular nature of the relations and forces that link them is revealed in that which appears to be, according to Granger, a "comprehensive description." At its best, this description provides an explanation. This comprehensive description presumes a theory by which the singularity of these relationships and constraints can be understood and determined, because they reveal themselves on an abstract level, that of the properties of these relationships and forces that link the parts to the whole.

The case study has proven to be in complete harmony with the three key words that characterize any qualitative method: describing, understanding, and explaining. Such a study is best able to describe and understand the case under investigation. This study is considered to be a superior method of description, and the choices and tactics that define it also precisely define the process of transformation from local to global. This ensures the general applicability of the explanation.

Such general applicability thus results from the set of methodological qualities in the selected case, and the rigor with which the study, or the analysis resulting from this case, is conducted. Robert K. Yin (1989a), in a noteworthy text, has introduced a distinction between analytical generality and statistical generality. He believes that the case study, "like the experiment, does not represent a 'sample,' and the investigator's goal is to expand and generalize theories (analytic generalization) and not to enumerate frequencies (statistical generalization)" (Yin, 1989a, p. 21).

In analytic generalization, the investigator is striving to generalize a particular set of results to some broader theory. However, the generalization is not automatic. A theory must be tested through replications of the findings in a second or even a third [experiment], where the theory had specified that the same results should occur. (p. 44)

The generality of the case study, like any other laboratory test, is relative to the methodological value of the test process involved in the experiment itself, and "holds until proved otherwise," as the scientists put it. The methodological value of the experimental devices in the case study is essentially based on (a) the quality of strategies selected in defining the object of study and in the selection of the social unit that makes up the ideal vantage point from which to understand it; as well as (b) the methodological rigor displayed in the description of this subject in the form of a sociological analysis that can be understood in action. This analysis must therefore be properly reproduced to test its generality through other cases selected on the basis of the same object of study and that incorporate the same strategic qualities, so that it may be understood.

Notes

1. In addition to the previously cited article by Houle (1986), see Godelier (1978, 1984), where he asked the following question: "If ideology is defined as an illusion or falsehood, for whom is it illusory or false? Not for those who believe in it and who cling to this ideology as the sole truth and which determines their awareness of the world." These remarks by Godelier are much more subtle than those noted in the text on the subject of Lévi-Strauss's structuralism.

2. As noted in previous remarks, anthropologists benefited from the fact that the societies that served as the field of choice for their monographs were, at that time, homogeneous and relatively simple.

4. THE CASE STUDY:
PRACTICAL COMMENTS AND GUIDANCE

We shall conclude with a few practical comments on the case study, and provide a guide of how to best define the correct process involved in this approach. The advice and guidance are straightforward; their sole ambition is to illustrate what has just been discussed, in terms of the historical and methodological considerations pertaining to the case study. They are also intended to enhance the bibliography that appears in the following section of this work. These comments and this guide make special reference to, if not recommend, various works, enabling the reader to probe deeper into issues that have been raised. A review of certain classic case studies, particularly works from the Chicago School, both "old" and "new," provides some examples illustrating issues discussed in the guide and in the practical comments.

Definition of the Object of Study

It is never simple, in sociology, to define the object of study in a way that will explain a social issue or a phenomenon. This is so whatever approach may be selected. The same applies to case studies. In fact, the difficulty is perhaps even greater when the case study is advocated for this purpose. Although the case study is an inductive approach, perhaps even the ideal inductive approach, that does not mean the definition of the object is a matter of chance or conjecture. This may be surprising, because it runs counter to the perception that the case study lacks a precise subject of investigation as its point of departure. Such a definition of the object may even be said to be established during the course of the study. It may assert itself, particularly if the case study is a long-term field study, like those conducted by anthropologists since the time of Malinowski, with exotic societies as the field of preference. By establishing increasingly close ties with the field, the researcher will ultimately be able to define the object of study. The examples of studies by Miner and Hughes, however, demonstrate the contrary. The case study tradition these studies inspired in the interactionist perspective also tend to show that the researcher has carefully and previously defined the object of study that gives rise to the case study. Whether the study concerns pot smokers or the jazz musicians in Becker's (1963) *Outsiders*, such studies start off with a clearly defined subject, in these cases patterns of behavior violating the accepted standard of a particular social group or institution.

Researchers choose a field because they specifically intend to study a special subject, and this field would appear to be such an ideal place to observe it that the definition of the object is often confused with that of the field, or of the case itself. It is thus appropriate to distinguish between the object of study and the selected case study for purposes of observation, while at the same time clearly defining the former. Such a definition is clearly formulated insofar as it is associated with the goal of sociology, which is simply, as is often said, "to explain the social by the social." This expression may appear self-evident. However, it still gives rise to endless discussions about whether a sociological "fact" should be perceived as interactions between individuals, common patterns of behavior, social structures, or social relationships. This list can continue to grow, as noted at the beginning of this work. Nonetheless, and without a definitive answer for the moment, we should agree that any object being investigated by sociology must be defined in response to these apparently mundane questions:

42

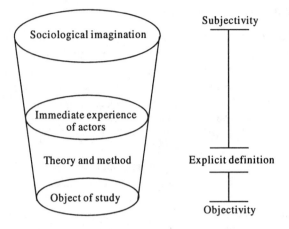

Figure 4.1. Definition of the Object of Study

How does society generate the problem or phenomenon under consideration by the study? In what way is this problem or phenomenon determined socially? The researcher, in this case the sociologist, should always be guided by this question in defining the object of study. Such a definition is strictly of his or her own making. Such a definition may not be imposed by the field, or by key informants. In other words, it may not directly arise from remarks collected in the field. It is the researcher's personal duty to define this object, and this definition must demonstrate that the sociological point of view shall henceforth play a role.

Does this mean that the researcher's subjectivity will enter into the study to the extent that the required objectivity has been compromised? Certainly, the researcher's subjectivity will intervene, and must intervene, to produce a definition of the object. This definition involves breaking down the personal experiences of the actors, as described above. The process will enable the object to be perceived in a more limited, but precise, manner as a social fact, as is illustrated by Figure 4.1.

The researcher's subjectivity does intervene, but to the extent this intervention is clearly stated, it then becomes objectified into an object that is clearly the sociologist's point of view, or more precisely, the sociological point of view. This explanation is constructed in terms of sociological methodology and theory; that is, it is put into conceptual and operative terms resulting from methodological tactics and concepts recommended for defining the object. Although these terms may impose the desired rigor, they do not necessarily impede the sociological imagination. On the contrary, if this imagination fails to take on the sociological perspective in any way, one that is essentially determined by its objective, the definition of an object of study in sociology may correspond with the particularly incisive statement of Zonabend (1992), who states says that objectivity and subjectivity cannot be contrasted: "We must be aware that the most rigorous objectivity is only possible through the most intrepid subjectivity" (p. 53).

Selecting the Ideal Case to Grasp the Object of Study

Although the objectivity displayed in the definition of the object of study is only possible through the most intrepid subjectivity, this is the only way case selection can be defined, if we are to understand this object. The sociological imagination expresses itself though this choice, on a purely methodological level. This does not, however, mean that it does so according to a methodological plan inspired by Le Play's suggestion that the condition of a society can be revealed through the systematic study of an appropriately chosen microsocial unit (Kalaora & Savoye, 1989). Although this choice reveals the preferred methodological tactics for understanding the object of study, these must also be defined. This is done by detailing the methodological qualities assigned to the chosen case, based on the selected object to explain "the state of a society," as Le Play put it. In other words, this involves a social issue or phenomenon. The previously considered Chicago School case studies provide irrefutable examples of such clear definitions, although today they might look like a worthless methodological patchwork. On the contrary, Hughes's choice of Drummondville proved a perfectly strategic choice because it permitted study of the ethnic division of labor as it was manifested not only in that town, but throughout French-Canadian society. His remarks were clear from this point of view and he stipulated them at the outset:

> The current changes in French Canadian life and problems are those of concurrent industrialization and urbanization, both brought about by expansion of the Anglo-American world. The completely rural parish described by Horace Miner in his *St. Denis, a French-Canadian Parish* (Chicago: University of Chicago Press, 1939) may be taken as the prototype of Quebec

communities as yet scarcely affected by these changes. Montreal, the metropolis of Quebec and of all Canada, represents the other extreme. This book deals mainly with a community which stands between these extremes, a smaller town recently enlivened and disturbed by the establishment of a number of large new industries, all started and managed by English-speaking people sent there for the purpose. The facts, relationships, and changes discovered in this community are also to be found in many others. (Hughes, 1943, p. 10)

Although this choice may, at first glance, appear to be dictated by inherently empirical considerations, Hughes's remarks clearly indicated that he relied on a methodological strategy to which he subscribed in explaining French Canada in transition. This methodological strategy results from a theory, an *initial theory*, to be more precise, the formulation of which is revealed by this strategy. *Initial theory* means the initial idea that a researcher had of the perceived social issue or phenomenon. This initial idea is mainly presented in the definition of the object, and this definition must have been determined within the framework of sociology, for example, urban ecology. In the case of Hughes, this defined the framework of a sociological perspective.

In this sense, case selection is theoretical; that is, it is based on sociological theory. That is why we should specify that a selected case is sociologically representative, and not just representative of a statistical point of view. In terms of Yin's distinction, the selected case is not representative because of the observed frequency at which a social issue or phenomenon occurs. It is representative in terms of an initial sociological theory, which presents it as the selected observation point for an object of study. An analysis of this object will establish how general it is. This generality is "analytic," as Yin (1989a, p. 21) so aptly put it. It is analytic in the sense that it is derived from the analysis of the case that is presented as the preferred vantage point. Thus, the representativeness of the case is relative to the methodological qualities attributed to it. The definition of the case permits an assessment of its generality in view of results of the analysis it has made possible.

We accordingly cannot overemphasize the importance of broadly defining case selection. More precisely, we must explain the various methodological tactics prevailing in the strategic selection of a case. This can easily be modeled on detailed explanations about laboratory equipment and test procedures, as in the experimental sciences, and which serve as a basis for the generality of the results produced by this method.

The Wealth of Empirical Materials

The case study is an in-depth investigation. It accordingly uses different methods to collect various kinds of information and to make observations. These are the empirical materials through which the object of study will be understood. The case study is thus based on a great wealth of empirical materials, notably because of their variety. Most writings on the case study method are in agreement with this. Nonetheless, this wide variety of empirical materials presents analytical problems.

This variety appears as much in the diversity of the empirical materials as in their treatment. These may be news reports, official documents, remarks in context, personal writings, literary works such as novels, and so forth. The case study thus considers materials of different origins, which are produced by different types of knowledge. Informants' remarks express direct knowledge, whereas news reports involve a more elaborate form of knowledge (although this characterization is not meant to denigrate the personal knowledge revealed by what informants say). Official documents from political authorities, for example, produce a knowledge that lends itself to their inherently administrative purposes, whereas fiction is the product or result of an elaboration of knowledge that obeys narrative rules.

The analysis of all these materials poses serious problems, which are analogous to the kinds of incompatibilities that exist between documents produced in PC and Macintosh systems. In other words, how can empirical materials be used in an analysis aimed at a sociological, not to say scientific, knowledge if they have been treated differently, in accordance with their different intellectual origins?

Epistemology, particularly that of the French school (Granger, 1988; Houle, 1986) provides an initial answer to this question. To begin with, the object of study must be described as it is empirically defined, or, better yet, as it is constructed within these various materials. The definition of this object must be inherently sociological; that is, it must be a definition provided by the researcher that corresponds to the aim of the study, and "to explain the social by the social." The object of study must thus be demonstrated as it is constructed within the set of empirical materials, such as official documents, informants' remarks, and so forth. Such demonstration actually requires that the form of the selected material be "deconstructed," so that the researcher's object may be produced and constructed in a sociological form. This form is that of a sociological study that depicts sociology as a form of specific, scientific knowledge.

Without going into detail on its characterization as a form of knowledge, science can be unequivocally understood as: "an attempt to rationalize facts with a knowledge that can be demonstrated" (Granger, 1986, p. 114). In this sense, the depth of the description of the case study naturally provides this demonstration, because it facilitates a clear understanding of what the object of study refers to in the materials. This transformation from the object of study, defined from a sociological perspective, to its empirical construction within these materials is thus essentially determined in the definition of the object under analysis. The object under analysis is the object on which the analysis is based within the selected materials. It is presented in the appropriate form for each set of materials. The in-depth description for which the case study is known thus provides a demonstrable means of understanding how the elements of materials under analysis, which appear in a specific form, specifically refer to the object of study, an object that has been defined from a sociological perspective.

Practically speaking, it is thus appropriate to determine rigorously the object of study in the transformation from the theoretical definition of the object of study to its empirical construction within the selected materials. The variety of these materials will ensure the depth of the case study. The rigor of the definition of the object under analysis depends here on the depth of the description characteristic of the case study approach.

Problems in the Writing

By using materials of different origins and providing the in-depth analysis that process implies, the case study can clearly illustrate problems in both the literature and, more generally, the language, of sociology, or for that matter, in the other social sciences. It is only infrequently noted that sociology is, first and foremost, work created by language, about language, and yielding language (see Houle, 1986). And yet, this discipline mobilizes tools (concepts, etc.) created by the language, and acting on the language. Empirical materials are created out of them (informants' remarks, official documents, news reports, etc.). This serves to produce knowledge "of the social by the social." Its form is essentially generated through language. Under such circumstances, we must consider the problem of language, beginning with its most direct manifestation, writing (Van Maanen, 1988).

The previously discussed transformation from the theoretical definition of the object of study to its empirical construction within the selected materials, provides a clear outline, using the case study approach. Because such a study gives an in-depth description, it provides an understanding, in action, of the way the language of the empirical materials is shaped into another language, that of sociology. In the same vein, the theoretical construction of empirical materials may thus be directly understood within an analysis. The description that defines the depth of this analysis also reveals its full scope. In other words, the description presents this theoretical construction in action, and thus provides a grasp of the elements and procedures that are primarily defined in the language. The description is thus not strictly an empirical one, as it is usually perceived. It would be more appropriate to speak of a descriptive theory, inasmuch as the description proves to be an analysis or an object of study appearing in the form of empirical materials and produced as a theory whose form is first apparent in language, and, more particularly, in the use made of it from a sociological perspective.

What special quality does language, as influenced by the sociological perspective, have? If sociology is a science, the language that describes it must, by definition, be univocal. Epistemology emphasizes this quality of language with respect to all science. Science expresses itself as a form of knowledge seeking clarity and rigor. The univocality of its language is the first illustration of this feature. The same principle applies to sociology. Sociology can only precisely determine a specific analytic perspective, as it hopes to do, if the language used to define the tools and the operations made possible by them is univocal. This requirement is particularly important in sociology, because its characteristic analysis is actually based (using the case study as an example) on a type of intersection. This intersection occurs between the common language that describes the form of the object of study in terms of the selected empirical materials, and the language that gives form to the tools and the operations from the sociological perspective.

A review of the classical works of the Chicago School shows this ongoing concern for clearly distinguishing common language from that used for analytical purposes. The professional studies of Hughes (1958/ 1981) thus provide a sort of comparative approach to language in which "analytical categories free from value judgments and from the categories used by workers themselves (or by their employers) for practical purposes [are defined]" (Chapoulie, 1986-1987, p. 278). More specifically, Hughes establishes a sort of play in the language that, by comparison, would make it possible to distinguish the language used in selected empirical materials (interviews, in this case) from that used for the sociological analysis aimed at understanding a specific object of study.

Although sociological language must meet the demands of univocality, writing in itself must comply with three qualities of rigor: (a) The writing must be free of any stylistic features eliciting other forms of knowledge, such as literature. (b) Sociological writing must include features of demonstrable knowledge and thus be analogous to the formulas and symbols of chemistry (e.g., $2H_2 + O_2 = 2H_2O$). Although it cannot actually produce such expressions, sociological style should still be concise and avoid plays on words that could suggest any ambiguity. And (c), the sociological perspective expressed in its writings should accordingly display an irreducibility of language. This irreducibility should facilitate understanding and referencing throughout the sociological analysis of the case study.

Constructing the Explanation

The explanation arrived at by the case study cannot depend on the qualities of sociological writing alone, although it is based on them. This explanation, like any other sociological explanation or, for that matter, any scientific explanation, must be accurately and completely transmissible in a written statement. Granger (1989) wrote, "There is no scientific knowledge that cannot be expressed by a symbolic system which can be communicated through a language, in contrast to certain essentially imitative fields of knowledge, which pertain to art" (p. 13). Accordingly, the case study must produce an explanation that cannot refer to or suggest any intuitive, tacit, and imitative fields of knowledge that this study cannot provide and contain within a written statement. The theoretical and methodological foundations of the explanation resulting from the case study may thus be clearly understood through the depth of description of the object of study, as was previously emphasized.

Moreover, this explanation must be presented as new information. The case study must not conclude in a systematization of field information, presented as an explanation. In other words, such a study must not be a restatement of information that has been collected and arranged by the written word to give it a systematic appearance. The explanation must provide information that, although based on the analysis of field information, transcends this information because of the sociological perspective prevailing over the case study. This is possible because this explanation, like any scientific explanation, must appear in an abstract form.

By *abstract form* we do not mean that the explanation must be difficult to understand or appear in some esoteric form, as is commonly believed. The explanation is abstract in that it must be constructed in a theoretical language, that of sociology. Because of its abstract form, it is this language that makes it possible for the explanation to become abstracted, and to "detach itself," which would be a better way of putting it, from the direct point of view contained in field information, thus illustrating this information from the sociological perspective.

In reducing epistemological considerations regarding the language of science, including sociology, to the extreme, it is recognized that the abstraction necessary to achieve this goal is produced primarily through a refinement of the terms and procedures involved in the natural language (Granger, 1979). In other words, abstraction is produced by replacing the terms and procedures that the natural language already possesses with the terms and procedures inherent in sociology and that result from its objectives. This substitution must comply with the principle of univocality, which must be sought in establishing the sociological language and writing. A very simple example will illustrate this. Although the expression "upper middle class" is currently used to designate those who are well off, those who have a fortune, or those whose lives are marked by luxury (and there is no end to the meanings that could be assigned to this term), for Marx it would simply mean "those who own the means of production," the implementation of which comes under his theory of capital and labor that is aimed at explaining capitalist society. This may be represented in Figure 4.2, which is intended to provide a detailed view of the natural, direct language.

The abstraction produced by the refinement of natural language may be understood in action, in the case study. This may be done precisely because of the depth of the description involved in such a study. In this sense, as previously emphasized, this description is a descriptive theory, because it is based on the abstract level resulting from this refinement of the natural language that involves replacing its immediately significant attributes with univocal and operative significant attributes falling within the scope of sociology.

The explanation produced by the case study must, therefore, be based on this abstract level made possible by the refinement of natural language, and must not deviate from this course. It will then be possible to understand how and why field information used to describe the case is forged

50

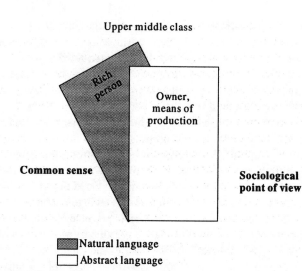

Upper middle class

Rich person

Owner, means of production

Common sense

Sociological point of view

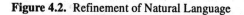
Natural language
Abstract language

Figure 4.2. Refinement of Natural Language

into an explanation in which the sociological perspective is manifest. The case study thus subscribes to an attempt to rationalize facts with a knowledge that can be demonstrated, characteristic of the science sociology aspires to be.

5. THEMATIC BIBLIOGRAPHY
FOR THE CASE STUDY

An examination of the case study must necessarily be coupled with a bibliography of the research conducted in this area of qualitative methods that, although certainly a part of sociology and anthropology, is also used in such areas as psychology, education, and the administrative sciences. The foregoing discussion enabled us to see the case study as a rigorous approach that, based on a carefully chosen case, yields a generally applicable explanation. It must be recognized that this definition of the case study does not correspond to the conception that sees in the case study only an approach confined to local "specific" cases, which, due to their poor representativeness, can only be seen as exploratory.

The bibliography presented on the following pages corresponds to the definition proposed in the first part of this discussion. It takes up the main themes covered, which were essentially theoretical and methodological considerations that, although applicable to the case study, may be extended to the sociological approach in general. The problem of defining the object of study or determining the most appropriate case for looking at it representatively, and the problem of the objectivity required in this type of observation or the analytical rigor that will lead to an explanation, are common to any approach selected to satisfy the aim of sociology, which is to "explain the social by the social." The presentation of this bibliography in fact follows the order of the themes presented in the chapters in the first part of this book.

Furthermore, the accent is on methodological writings on the case study. It should be noted, however, that the bibliography presented here accordingly makes no claim to be an inventory of all the case studies carried out in sociology or any other field, with the exception of universally recognized classic cases. It mainly contains the titles of publications, articles, or books that have appeared in English or French over the past 20 years in sociology and the other social sciences. Works from other fields, such as psychology, administration, and so forth, are included, provided they are of a methodological nature or deal with some aspect of the case study method.

This bibliography has been compiled on the basis of searches in the following computerized data bases and printed indexes:

- *Francis* (Centre National de la Recherche Scientifique, Paris)
- *Sociofile*
- *Bulletin signalétique* (sociology, ethnology, and philosophy)
- *Sociological Abstracts*
- *Historical Abstracts*

Each of the publications for which a bibliographical record was found in these databases and indexes was examined before being selected or rejected. The bibliography of each publication was also carefully consulted, thus leading us to other bibliographical references.

The bibliography of a field as vast as the case study, considered in its various theoretical and practical aspects, which are in turn linked to qualitative methods in sociology, the other social sciences and other fields, can hardly be claim to be comprehensive. A serious effort was made, however, to seek out the essential information in terms of positions put forward in relation to qualities of the case study in its capacity to explain, which must be the aim of sociology as a social science and the science of social phenomena. It is our hope that this bibliography, while mirroring the positions advanced in this study, will nevertheless also reflect the various other positions taken with respect to the case study and encourage readers to obtain more information on them.

CONTENTS OF THE THEMATIC BIBLIOGRAPHY FOR THE CASE STUDY

A. HISTORY OF THE CASE STUDY APPROACH: FRENCH AND AMERICAN SCHOOLS

Frédéric Le Play School

1. METHODOLOGICAL CONTRIBUTIONS OF THE LE PLAY SCHOOL

Bureau, P. (1926). *La science des moeurs: introduction à la méthode sociologique* [The science of customs: Introduction to the sociological method] (2nd ed.). Paris: Bloud et Gay.
Cochin, A. (1856). *Les ouvriers européens: résumé de la méthode et des observations de monsieur Le Play* [European workers: A summary of Le Play's method and observations]. Paris: Duniol.
Curzon, E. P. de. (1889). *Frédéric Le Play: sa méthode, sa doctrine, son œuvre, son esprit d'après ses écrits et sa correspondance* [Frédéric Le Play: His method, his philosophy, his work, his thoughts according to his writings and his letters]. Paris: H. Oudin.

Descamps, P. (1912-1919). Cours de méthode de science sociale [Social sciences methodological lessons]. *La science sociale* (1912, November; 1913, November; 1914, December; 1918, May; 1919, November).

Desmolins, E. (1881). L'enquête permanente [The permanent inquiry]. *La réforme sociale*, 2, 5-6.

Du Maroussem, P. (1900). *Les enquêtes: Pratique et théorie* [Inquiries: Practice and theory]. Paris: Alcan.

Le Play, F. (1855). *Les ouvriers européens* [European workers]. Paris: Imprimerie impériale.

Le Play, F. (1882). *Instruction sur la méthode d'observation dite des monographies de famille* [Instruction in the observation of social facts according to the Le Play method of family monographs]. Paris: A. J. Focillon. (Original work published 1862)

Le Play, F. (1906). *F. Le Play d'après lui-même: vie, méthode, doctrine: Notices et morceaux choisis* [Frédéric Le Play by himself: His life, method, philosophy: Selected notes and papers]. Paris: Giard et Brière.

Le Play, F. (1947). *Textes choisis* [Selected papers]. Paris: Dalloz.

Le Play, F. (1983). *Ouvriers des deux mondes: études publiées par la Société d'Économie Sociale à partir de 1856 sous la direction de Frédéric Le Play* [Workers of both worlds: Studies published from 1856 by the Société d'Économie Sociale, with Frédéric Le Play acting as editor]. Thomery, France: À l'enseigne de l'arbre verdoyant Éditeur. (Original work published 1857)

Le Play, F. (1989). *La méthode sociale* [The social method]. Paris: Méridiens-Klincksieck. (Original work published 1879)

Prieur, P. (1986, May). Introduction au cours de méthode d'observation sociale [Introduction to the social observation lesson]. *La science sociale*, pp. 393-410.

Tourville, H. de. (1886). La science sociale est-elle une science? [Is social science really a science?]. *La science sociale*, January, 9-21; February, 97-109; April, 289-304; December, 493-516.

2. ON LE PLAY SCHOOL

Arnault, F. (1984). Frédéric Le Play, de la métallurgie à la science sociale. [Frédéric Le Play, from the steel industry to the social science]. *Revue française de sociologie*, 25, 437-457.

Assier-Andrieu, L. (1984). Le Play et la famille souche des Pyrénées: politique, juridisme et science sociale [Le Play and the Pyrenees' stem family: Politics, laws and social science]. *Annales E.S.C.*, 39(3), 495-512.

Bodard-Silver, C. (Ed.). (1982). *Frédéric Le Play: On family, work and social change*. Chicago: University of Chicago Press.

Brooke, M. (1970). *Le Play: Engineer and social scientist*. London: Longmann.

Clement, M. (1957). Quelques remarques sur la méthodologie sociale de Le Play [Some notes on Le Play's social methodology]. In R. Grand (Ed.), *Recueil d'études sociales* [Collection of social studies] (pp. 21-28). Paris: Éditions A. et J. Picard et Cie.

Dauphin, C., & Pezerat, P. (1975). Les consommateurs populaires dans la seconde moitié du XIXe siècle à travers les monographies de l'École de Le Play. [Working class consumers during the second half of the 19th century, as seen through Le Play's School Monographs]. *Annales E.S.C.*, 2-3, 537-552.

Kalaora, B., & Savoye, A. (1985). La mutation du mouvement le playsien [Changes in the Le Playsian movement]. *Revue française de sociologie*, 26, 257-276.

55

Kalaora, B., & Savoye, A. (1989). *Les inventeurs oubliés* [The forgotten inventors]. Paris: Champ Vallon.

Polin, R. (1938). Monographie et synthèse d'après Le Play [Monograph and synthesis according to Le Play]. In *Les convergences des sciences sociales et l'esprit international* [Social sciences convergences and the international context] (pp. 246-251). Paris: Hartmann.

Savoye, A. (1981). Les continuateurs de Le Play au tournant du siècle [Le Play's followers at the turn of the century]. *Revue française de sociologie, 22,* 315-344.

Savoye, A. (1987). Sociologie et ingéniérie sociale [Sociology and social engineering]. *Milieux, 28,* 6-15.

Savoye, A. (Ed.). (1989). Le Play. *Sociétés, 23*(May).

Tomasi, L. (1989). L'influence de Le Play sur la sociologie américaine [The influence of Le Play on American sociology]. *Sociétés, 23,* 37-39.

Treanton, J.-R. (1984). Faut-il exhumer Le Play? Ou les héritiers abusifs [Must we dig up Le Play's legacy? The misusing heirs]. *Revue française de sociologie, 25,* 458-483.

Chicago School

1. METHODOLOGICAL CONTRIBUTIONS OF THE CHICAGO SCHOOL

Burgess, E. W. (1927). Statistics and case studies as methods of social research. *Sociology and Social Research, 12,* 103-120.

Burgess, E. W. (1928). What social case studies records should contain to be useful for sociological interpretation. *Social Forces, 6,* 524-532.

Burgess, E. W. (1941). An experiment in the standardization of the case study method. *Sociometry, 4,* 329-348.

Burgess, E. W. (Ed.). (1985). *Strategies of field research.* Lewes, UK: Falmer.

Cooley, C. H. (1927). Case study of small institutions as a method of research. *Publications of the American Sociological Society, 22,* 123-132.

Cresey, P. G. (1983). A comparison of the roles of the "sociological stranger" and the "anonymous stranger" in field research. *Urban Life, 12,* 102-120.

Hughes, E. C. (1959). The study of occupations. In R. K. Merton, L. Broom, & L. S. Cottrel (Eds.), *Sociology today* (pp. 442-458). New York: Basic Books.

Hughes, E. C. (1960). Introduction: The place of field work in the social research. In B. Junker, *Field work: An introduction to the social science* (pp. v-xv). Chicago: University of Chicago Press.

Hughes, E. C. (1970). The humble and the proud: The comparative studies of occupations. *The Sociological Quarterly, 11*(2), 147-156.

Hughes, E. C. (1970). Teaching as field work. *American Sociologist, 5*(1), 13-18.

Hughes, E. C. (1971). *The sociological eye: Selected papers.* Chicago: Aldine.

Hughes, E. C. (1974). Who studies whom? *Human Organization, 33*(4), 327-334.

Hughes, E. C., & Benney, M. (1956). Of sociology and the interview: Editorial preface. *American Journal of Sociology, 62,* 137-142.

Palmer, V. (1928). *Field studies in sociology: A student's manual.* Chicago: University of Chicago Press.

Park, R. E. (1921). The city as a social laboratory. In T. V. Smith & L. D. White (Eds.), *Chicago: An experiment in social science research* (pp. 1-19). Chicago: University of Chicago Press.

56

Park, R. E. (1930). Murder and the case study method. *American Journal of Sociology, 36*, 447-454.

Park, R. E. (1955). *Society*. Glencoe, IL: Free Press.

Park, R. E., & Burgess, E. W. (Eds.). (1969). *Introduction to the science of sociology* (3rd ed.). Chicago: University of Chicago Press.

Shaw, C. A. (1926). Case study method. *Publications of the American Sociological Society, 21*, 149-157.

Znaniecki, F. (1934). *The method of sociology*. New York: Farrar & Rinehart.

2. METHODOLOGICAL CONTRIBUTIONS OF THE SECOND CHICAGO SCHOOLS

Becker, H. S. (1934). Culture case study and ideal-typical method. *Social Forces, 12*(3), 399-405.

Becker, H. S. (1954). A note on interviewing tactics. *Human Organization, 12*(4), 31-32.

Becker, H. S. (1956). Interviewing medical students. *American Journal of Sociology, 62*, 199-201.

Becker, H. S. (1958). Problems of inference and proof in participant observation. *American Sociological Review, 23*(6), 652-660.

Becker, H. S. (1964). Problems in the publication of field studies. In A. J. Vidich, J. Bensman, & M. R. Stein (Eds.), *Reflections on community studies* (pp. 267-284). New York: John Wiley.

Becker, H. S. (1968). Social observation and social case studies. In *International encyclopedia of the social sciences* (Vol. 11, pp. 232-238). London: Collier-Macmillan.

Becker, H. S. (1970a). Life history and the scientific mosaic. In H. S. Becker, *Sociological work: Method and substance* (pp. 63-73). Chicago: Aldine.

Becker, H. S. (1970b). *Sociological work: Method and substance*. Chicago: Aldine.

Becker, H. S., & Geer, B. (1957). Participant observation and interviewing: A comparison. *Human Organization, 16*(3), 28-32.

Becker, H. S., & Geer, B. (1958). Participant observation and interviewing: A rejoinder. *Human Organization, 17*(2), 39-40.

Becker, H. S., & Geer, B. (1960). Participant observation: The analysis of qualitative field data. In R. N. Adams & J. J. Preiss (Eds.), *Human organization research: Field relations and techniques* (pp. 267-289). Homewood, IL: Dorsey.

Cicourel, A. V. (1964). *Method and measurement in sociology*. New York: Free Press.

Whyte, W. F. (1951). Observation field methods. In M. Vahoda, M. Deutsch, & S. W. Cook (Eds.), *Research methods in social relations* (Vol. 2, pp. 493-513). New York: Holt.

Whyte, W. F., & King-Whyte, K. (1984). *Learning from the field: A guide from experience*. Beverly Hills, CA: Sage.

3. CASE STUDIES AND COMMUNITY STUDIES FROM THE FIRST AND THE SECOND CHICAGO SCHOOLS

Anderson, N. (1923). *The hobo: The sociology of the homeless man*. Chicago: University of Chicago Press.

Becker, H. S. (1963). *Outsiders*. New York: Free Press.

Becker, H. S., Geer, B., & Hughes, E. C. (1968). *Making the grade: The academic side of college life*. New York: John Wiley.

Becker, H. S., Geer, B., Hughes, E. C., & Strauss, A. (1961). *Boys in white: Student culture in medical school.* Chicago: University of Chicago Press.

Burleigh, D. A., & Gardner, M. (1941). *Deep South.* Chicago: University of Chicago Press.

Cavan, R. S. (1928). *Suicide.* Chicago: University of Chicago Press.

Cicourel, A. V. (1968). *The social organization of juvenile justice.* New York: John Wiley.

Cressey, P. G. (1932). *The taxi-dance hall.* Chicago: University of Chicago Press.

Faris, R.E.L., & Dunham, H. W. (1965). *Mental disorders in urban areas.* Chicago: University of Chicago Press.

Frazier, F. E. (1939). *The Negro family in the United States.* Chicago: University of Chicago Press.

Hughes, E. C. (1943). *French Canada in transition.* Chicago: University of Chicago Press.

Hughes, E. C. (1979). *The growth of an institution: The Chicago Real Estate Board* [Hughes's 1928 doctoral dissertation, Society for Social Research, Series II, Monograph 1]. New York: Arno.

Hughes, E. C. (1981). *Men and their work.* Westport, CT: Greenwood. (Original work published 1958)

Hughes, E. C., McGill-Hughes, H., & Deutscher, I. (1958). *Twenty thousand nurses tell their story.* Philadelphia: J. B. Lippincott.

Liebow, E. (1967). *Tally's corner: A study of Negro streetcorner men.* Boston: Little, Brown.

Miner, H. (1939). *Saint-Denis, a French-Canadian parish.* Chicago: University of Chicago Press.

Park, R. E. (1950). *Race and culture.* Glencoe, IL: Free Press.

Park, R. E. (1952). *Human communities: The city and human ecology.* New York: Free Press.

Park, R. E., Burgess, E. W., & McKenzie, R. (1925). *The city.* Chicago: University of Chicago Press.

Redfield, R. (1930). *Topaztlan, a Mexican village.* Chicago: University of Chicago Press.

Redfield, R. (1941). *The folk culture of Yucatan.* Chicago: University of Chicago Press.

Redfield, R. (1956). *The little community.* Chicago: University of Chicago Press.

Shaw, C. A. (1930). *The jackroller: A delinquent boy's own story.* Chicago: University of Chicago Press.

Shaw, C. A. (1931). *The natural history of a delinquent career.* Chicago: University of Chicago Press.

Shaw, C. A. (1938). *Brothers in crime.* Chicago: University of Chicago Press.

Shaw, C. A., & McKay, H. D. (1939). *Social factors in juvenile delinquency.* Washington, DC: Government Printing Office.

Shaw, C. A., & McKay, H. D. (1942). *Juvenile delinquency and urban areas.* Chicago: University of Chicago Press.

Sutherland, E. H. (1937). *The professional thief.* Chicago: University of Chicago Press.

Sutherland, E. H. (1949). *White collar crime.* New York: Dryden.

Thomas, W. I., & Znaniecki, F. (1918-1920). *The Polish peasant in Europe and America* (5 vols.). Chicago: University of Chicago Press.

Trasher, F. M. (1927). *The gang: A study of 1313 gangs in Chicago.* Chicago: University of Chicago Press.

Warner, L. W. (1941, 1942, 1945, 1947, 1959). *Yankee city series* (5 vols.). New Haven, CT: Yale University Press.

Wirth, L. (1928). *The ghetto.* Chicago: University of Chicago Press.

Zorbaugh, H. H. (1929). *The gold coast and the slum.* Chicago: University of Chicago Press.

4. ON THE FIRST AND THE SECOND CHICAGO SCHOOLS

Baker, P. J. (1974). The life histories of W. I. Thomas and Robert E. Park. *American Journal of Sociology, 79*, 243-260.

Baldwin, J. D. (1990). Advancing the Chicago school of pragmatic sociology: The life and work of Tamotsu Shibutani. *Sociological Inquiry, 60*(2), 115-126.

Ballis, L. B. (1986). The "Chicago School" of American sociology, symbolic interactionism, and race relations theory. In J. Rex & D. Mason (Eds.), *Theories of race and ethnic relations* (pp. 281-298). Cambridge: Cambridge University Press.

Bertaux, D. (1976). W. I. Thomas à Chicago, 1893-1920 [W. I. Thomas at Chicago, 1893-1920]. In *Histoires de vie ou récits de pratiques? Méthodologie de l'approche biographique en sociologie* [Life stories or everyday living accounts?: Methodology of the biographic approach in sociology] (pp. 1-86). Paris: CORDES.

Blumer, H. (1939). *An appraisal of Thomas and Znaniecki's* The Polish Peasant in Europe and America. New York: Social Science Research Council.

Breslau, D. (1988). Robert Park et l'écologie humaine [Robert Park and human ecology]. *Actes de la recherche en sciences sociales, 74*, 55-63.

Breslau, D. (1988). L'École de Chicago existe-t-elle? [Is there really a Chicago School?] *Actes de la recherche en sciences sociales, 74*, 64-65.

Breslau, D. (1990). La science, le sexisme et l'École de Chicago [Science, sexism, and the Chicago school]. *Actes de la recherche en sciences sociales, 85*, 94-95.

Bulmer, M. (1983). Chicago sociology and the society for social research: A comment. *Journal of the History of the Behavioral Sciences, 19*(4), 353-357.

Bulmer, M. (1983). The methodology of the taxi-dance hall. *Urban Life, 12*, 95-101.

Bulmer, M. (1984). *The Chicago School of sociology: Institutionalization, diversity and the rise of sociological research.* Chicago: University of Chicago Press.

Bulmer, M. (1985). The Chicago School of sociology: What made it a "school"? *The History of Sociology, 5*(2), 61-77.

Burns, L. R. (1980). The Chicago School and the study of organization environment relations. *Journal of the History of the Behavioral Sciences, 16*(4), 342-358.

Carey, J.-T. (1975). *Sociology and public affairs: The Chicago School.* Beverly Hills, CA: Sage.

Cavan, R. S. (1983). The Chicago School of sociology, 1918-1983. *Urban Life, 11*, 407-420.

Chapoulie, J.-M. (1985). Préface [Foreword]. In H. S. Becker, *Outsiders* (pp. 9-22). Paris: A-M Métaillé.

Chapoulie, J.-M. (1986-1987). Everett C. Hughes and the development of fieldwork in sociology. *Urban Life (Journal of Contemporary Ethnography), 15*(3-4), 259-298.

Debro, J. (1970). Dialogue with Howard Becker. *Issues in Criminology, 5*(2), 159-179.

Diner, S. J. (1975). Department and discipline: The department of sociology at the University of Chicago (1892-1920). *Minerva, 13*(4), 514-553.

Dubin, S. C., Bulmer, M., & Cressey, P. G. (1983). Dance halls. *Urban Life, 12*, 74-119.

Evans, R. (1986-1987). Sociological journals and the "decline" of Chicago sociology: 1929-1945. *History of Sociology, 6-7*(2-1-2), 109-130.

Farber, B. (1988). The human element: Sociology at Chicago. *Sociological Perspectives, 31*(3), 339-359.

Faris, R.E.L. (1967). *Chicago sociology 1920-1932.* Chicago: University of Chicago Press.

Faught, J. (1980). Presuppositions of the Chicago School in the work of Everett C. Hughes. *American Sociologist, 15*(2), 72-82.

Grafmeyer, Y., & Joseph, I. (Eds.). (1979). *L'École de Chicago: Naissance de l'écologie urbaine* [The Chicago School: The origins of urban ecology]. Paris: Aubier (Éditions du Champ urbain).

Haerle, R. K., Jr. (1991). William Isaac Thomas and the Helen Culver Fund for Race Psychology: The beginnings of scientific sociology at the University of Chicago, 1910-1913. *Journal of the History of the Behavioral Sciences, 27*(1), 21-41.

Hammersley, M. (1989). *Dilemma of the qualitative method: Blumer, Herbert and the Chicago School*. London: Routledge & Kegan Paul.

Harvey, L. (1986). The myths of the Chicago School. *Quality and Quantity, 20*(2-3), 191-217.

Harvey, L. (1987). *Myths of the Chicago School of sociology*. Brookfield, VT: Gower.

Hunter, A. (1980). Why Chicago? The rise of the Chicago School of urban social science. *American Behavioral Scientist, 24*, 215-227.

Hunter, A. (1983). The gold coast and the slum revisited: Paradoxes in replication research and the study of social change. *Urban Life, 11*, 461-476.

Kreiling, A. (1989). The Chicago School and community. *Critical Studies in Mass-Communication, 6*(3), 317-321.

Kurtz, L. R. (1984). *Evaluating Chicago sociology: A guide to the literature, with an annotated bibliography*. Chicago: University of Chicago Press.

Laperriére, A. (1982). Pour une construction empirique de la théorie: la nouvelle école de Chicago [An empirical construction of theory: The new Chicago School]. *Sociologie et sociétés, 14*(1), 31-41.

Lengermann, P.-M. (1988). Robert E. Park and the theoretical content of Chicago sociology: 1920-1940. *Sociological Inquiry, 58*(4), 361-377.

Lindstrom, F. B. (Ed.). (1988). Waving the flag for old Chicago. *Sociological Perspectives, 31*(3).

Lofland, L. H. (Ed.). (1980). Reminiscences of classic Chicago: The Blumer-Hughes talk. *Urban Life, 9*, 251-281.

Martin, P. Y., & Turner, B. A. (1986). Grounded theory and organizational research. *Journal of Applied Behavioral Science, 22*(2), 141-157.

Peneff, J. (1984). Notes sur E.C. Hughes et la pédagogie du fieldwork dans la sociologie américaine [Notes on E. C. Hughes and the teaching of fieldwork in American sociology]. *Sociologie du travail, 26*(2), 228-230.

Platt, J. (in press). Research methods and the second Chicago school. In G. A. Fine (Ed.), *The second Chicago school of sociology*.

Rémy, J., & Voyé, L. (1974). L'école de Chicago [The Chicago School]. In J. Rémy & L. Voyé, *La ville et l'urbanisation* [Urbanization and the city] (pp. 156-192). Belgium: Duculot.

Riesman, D. (1983). The legacy of Everett Hughes. *Contemporary Sociology, 12*, 477-481.

Simpson, I. H., & Chinoy, E. (1972). Symposium review on E. C. Hughes: Continuities in the sociology of Everett C. Hughes [Review of *The Sociological Eye*]. *Sociological Quarterly, 13*(4), 547-565.

Smith, D. (1988). *The Chicago School: A liberal critique of capitalism*. London: Macmillan Education.

Smith, T. V., & White, L. D. (Eds.). (1929). *Chicago: An experiment in social science research*. Chicago: University of Chicago Press.

Thomas, J. (1983). Chicago sociology: An introduction. *Urban Life, 11*, 387-395.

Thomas, J. (Ed.). (1983). The Chicago School: The tradition and the legacy. *Urban Life, 11*(4).

60

B. CASE STUDY APPROACH

Theoretical and Methodological Aspects

Adelman, L. (1991). Experiments, quasi-experiments and case-studies: A review of empirical methods for evaluating decision support systems. *IEEE Transactions on Systems, Man and Cybernetics, 21*(2), 293-301.

Amenta, E. (1991). Making the most of a case-study: Theories of the welfare-state and the American experience. *International Journal of Comparative Sociology, 32*(1-2), 172-194.

Augé, M., Bonte, P., Echard, N., Godelier, M., Gutwirth, J., Isambert, F., & Terrenoire, J.-P. (1978). Ethnologie et fait religieux: table ronde [Ethnology and religious facts: A debate]. *Revue française de sociologie, 19*, 571-584.

Ball, S. J. (1983). Case study research in education: Some notes and problems. In M. Hammersley (Ed.), *The ethnography of schooling: Methodological issues.* Driffield, UK: Nafferton.

Bennett, J. (1981). *Oral history and delinquency.* Chicago: University of Chicago Press.

Bleed, P. (1989). Objectivity, reflection and single case-studies: Comments on the effects of CRM. *Plains Anthropologist, 34*(124), 129-133.

Blumer, M. (1985). The rejuvenation of community studies? Neighbours, networks and policy. *Sociological Review, 33*(3), 430-448.

Bolgar, H. (1965). The case study method. In B. B. Wolman (Ed.), *Handbook of clinical psychology* (pp. 28-39). New York: McGraw-Hill.

Bromberger, C. (1991). Monographie [Monograph]. In P. Bonte & M. Izard (Eds.), *Dictionnaire de l'ethnologie et de l'anthropologie* [Dictionary of ethnology and anthropology] (pp. 484-486). Paris: PUF.

Bromley, D. B. (1986). *The case-study method in psychology and related disciplines.* New York: John Wiley.

Burgess, R. G. (1982). Styles of data analysis: Approaches and implications. In R. G. Burgess, *Field research: A source book and field manual* (pp. 235-238). London: Allen & Unwin.

Campbell, D. T. (1975). Degrees of freedom and case study. *Comparative Political Studies, 8*(2), 178-193.

Campbell, D. T., & Stanley, J. C. (1966). *Experimental and quasi experimental designs for research.* Chicago: Rand McNally.

Cernea, M. (1975). Le village roumain: Sociologie des recherches sur les communautés rurales [The Romanian village: The sociology of rural community researches]. *Archives internationales de sociologie de la coopération, 37*, 183-192.

Champagne, P. (1975). La restructuration de l'espace villageois [The restructuration of the village]. *Actes de la recherche en sciences sociales, 3*, 43-67.

Champagne, P. (1982). Statistique, monographie et groupes sociaux [Statistics, monographs, and social groups]. In *Études dédiées à Madeleine Grawitz* [Studies dedicated to Madeleine Grawitz] (pp. 3-16). Genève: Dalloz.

Charmes, J. (1973). La monographie villageoise comme démarche totalisante [The village monograph as an all-englobing process]. *Revue tiers-monde, 14*(55), 639-652.

Chiva, I. (1958). *Rural communities: Problems, methods and types of research.* Paris: UNESCO.

Colson, E. (1967). The intensive study of small sample communities. In A. L. Epstein (Ed.), *The craft of social anthropology* (pp. 3-16). London: Tavistock.

61

Copans, J. (1966). La monographie en question [The monograph in question]. *L'Homme,* *6*(3), 120-124.

Cresswell, R., & Godelier, M. (1976). La problématique anthropologique [The anthropological problematic]. In R. Cresswell & M. Godelier (Eds.), *Outils d'enquête et d'analyse anthropologique* [Tools for anthropological inquiry and analysis] (pp. 17-24). Paris: François Maspéro.

Crossley, M., & Vulliamy, G. (1984). Case-study research methods and comparative education. *Comparative Education, 20*(3), 193-207.

Cuvillier, A. (1967). La méthode monographique [The monographic method]. In A. Cuvillier, *Introduction à la sociologie* [An introduction to sociology] (pp. 115-122). Paris: Armand Colin.

De Bruyne, P., Herman, J., & de Schoutheete, M. (1974). Les études de cas [Case studies]. In P. De Bruyne, J. Herman, & M. de Schoutheete, *Dynamique de la recherche en sciences sociales* [The dynamics of research in social sciences] (pp. 211-214). Paris: PUF.

Dion, M. (1974). Des monographies en sociologie [Monographs in sociology]. In M. Jollivet (Ed.), *Les collectivités rurales françaises, t. 2: Sociétés paysannes ou luttes de classes au village?* [French rural communities: Vol. 2. Peasant societies or class struggle in the village?] (pp. 91-129). Paris: Armand Colin.

Eckstein, H. (1975). Case study and theory in political science. In F. I. Greenstein & N. W. Polsby (Eds.), *Handbook of political science: Strategies of inquiry* (Vol. 7, pp. 79-137). Reading, MA: Addison-Wesley.

Elmore, R. F. (1991). Towards rigor in reviews of multivocal literatures: Applying the exploratory case-study method—comment. *Review of Educational Research, 61*(3), 293-297.

Feagin, J. R., Drum, A., & Sjoberg, G. (1991). *A case for the case study.* Chapel Hill: University of North Carolina Press.

Foreman, P. B. (1948). The theory of case studies. *Social Forces, 26*(4), 408-419.

Fritz, J. M. (1985). *The clinical sociology handbook.* New York: Garland.

George, A. L. (1979). Case studies and theory development: The method of structured, focused comparison. In P. G. Lauren (Ed.), *Diplomacy: New approaches in history, theory and policy* (pp. 43-68). New York: Free Press.

Goode, W. J., & Hatt, P. K. (1952). The case study. In W. J. Goode & P. K. Hatt, *Methods in social research* (pp. 330-340). New York: McGraw-Hill.

Hakim, C. (1987). Case studies. In C. Hakim, *Research design: Strategies and choices in the design of social research* (pp. 61-75). London: Allen & Unwin.

Hamel, J. (1989). Pour la méthode de cas: considérations méthodologiques et perspectives générales [For the case study method: Methodological considerations and general perspectives]. *Anthropologie et sociétés, 13*(2), 59-72.

Hamel, J. (Ed.). (1992). The case method in sociology. *Current Sociology, 40*(1).

Hammersley, M. (1985). From ethnography to theory: A programme and paradigm for case study research in the sociology of education. *Sociology, 19*(2), 244-259.

Hammersley, M. (1986). *Case studies in classroom research: A reader.* Philadelphia: Open University Press.

Healey, W. (1923). The contribution of case studies to sociology. *Publications of the American Sociological Society, 13*, 147-155.

Hersen, M., & Barlow, D. H. (1976). *Single-case experimental designs: Strategies for studying behavior.* New York: Pergamon.

62

Hoover, D. W. (1989). Changing views of community studies: Middletown as a case study. *Journal of the History of the Behavioral Sciences, 25*(2), 111-124.

Kidder, L. (1981). Qualitative research and quasi-experimental frameworks. In M. Brewer & B. E. Collins (Eds.), *Scientific inquiry and the social sciences* (pp. 226-256). San Francisco: Jossey-Bass.

Lazarfeld, P. F., & Robinson, W. S. (1940). The quantification of case studies. *Journal of Applied Psychology, 24*, 817-825.

Leonard-Barton, D. (1990). A dual methodology for case studies: Synergistic use of a longitudinal single site with replicated multiple sites. *Organization Science, 1*(3), 248-266.

Lijphart, A. (1971). Comparative politics and the comparative method. *American Political Science Review, 65*(3), 682-693.

Lijpart, A. (1975). The comparable-cases strategy in comparative research. *Comparative Political Studies, 8*, 158-177.

Lucas, W. A. (1974). *The case survey method.* Santa Monica, CA: RAND.

Lundberg, G. A. (1941). Case studies vs. statistical methods: An issue based on misunderstanding. *Sociometry, 4*, 379-383.

Maget, M. (1989). Remarques sur le village comme cadre de recherches anthropologiques [Observations on the village as a setting for anthropological researches]. *Cahiers d'Économie et de Sociologie Rurales, 11*, 77-91.

Maho, J. (1980). Étudier et réétudier un village européen [Studying a European village over and again]. *Archives de l'observation continue du changement social, 3*, 41-55.

McClintock, C. C., Brannon, D., & Mood, S. M. (1979). Applying the logic of sample surveys to qualitative case studies: The case cluster method. *Administrative Science Quarterly, 24*(4), 612-629.

McDonagh, E. C. (1986). An approach to clinical sociology. *Clinical Sociology Review, 4*, 14-18.

Merriam, S. B. (1988). *Case study research in education: A qualitative approach.* San Francisco: Jossey-Bass.

Mitchell, J.-C. (1983). Case and situation analysis. *Sociology Review, 51*(2), 187-211.

Ogawa, R. T., & Malen, B. (1991). Towards rigor in reviews of multivocal literatures: Applying the exploratory case-study method. *Review of Educational Research, 61*(3), 265-286.

Pages, R. (1984). Cas (méthode des) [Case method]. In *Encyclopædia universalis* (Vol. 4, pp. 320-323). Paris: Encyclopædia Universalis France.

Platt, J. (1988). What can case studies do? In R. Burgess (Ed.), *Studies in qualitative methodology, 1*, 1-23.

Platt, J. (1992). "Case study" in American methodological thought. *Current Sociology, 40*(1), 17-48.

Queen, S. A. (1927). Round table on the case-study method of sociological research. *Publications of the American Sociological Society, 22*(128), 225-227.

Ragin, C., & Becker, H. S. (Eds.). (1992). *What is a case?: Exploring the foundations of social inquiry.* New York: Cambridge University Press.

Rosenblatt, P. C. (1981). Ethnographic case studies. In M. B. Brewer & B. E. Collins (Eds.), *Scientific inquiry and the social sciences* (pp. 194-225). San Francisco: Jossey-Bass.

Sanders, I. T. (1985). The social reconnaissance method of community study. *Research in Rural Sociology and Development, 2*, 235-255.

Sautter, G. (1961). L'étude régionale: réflexions sur la formule monographique en géographie humaine [The regional study: Some thoughts on the monographic approach in human geography]. *L'Homme, 1*(1), 77-89.

Simons, H. (1981). Conversation piece: The practice of interviewing in case study research. In C. Adelman (Ed.), *Uttering, muttering: Collecting, using and reporting talk for social and educational research*. London: Grant McIntyre.

Stake, R. C. (1978). The case study method in social inquiry. *Educational Researcher, 7*(2), 5-8.

Stein, H. (1952). Case method and the analysis of public administration. In H. Stein (Ed.), *Public administration and policy development* (pp. xiv-xx). New York: Harcourt Brace Jovanovich.

Stoecker, R. (1991). Evaluating and rethinking the case study. *Sociological Review, 39*(1), 88-112.

Tiévant, S. (1983). Les études de "communauté" et la ville: héritage et problèmes [Community studies and the city: Heritage and problems]. *Sociologie du travail, 25*(2), 243-257.

Trepper, T. S. (1990). In celebration of the case study. *Journal of Family Psychotherapy, 1*(1), 5-13.

Van Velson, J. (1967). The extended-case method and situational analysis. In A. L. Epstein (Ed.), *The craft of social anthropology* (pp. 129-152). London: Tavistock.

Vignet-Zunz, J. (1976). Présupposés scientifiques de la monographie rurale: une illustration [Scientific preconceptions of the rural monograph: An illustration]. *La Pensée, 187*, 67-73.

Vouvelle, M. (1985). De la biographie à l'étude de cas [From biography to case study]. *Sources: Travaux et histoire, 3-4*, 191-198.

Wieviorka, M. (1992). Case studies: History or sociology? In C. C. Ragin & H. S. Becker (Eds.), *What is a case? Exploring the foundations of social inquiry* (pp. 159-172). New York: Cambridge University Press.

Wilson, S. (1979). Explorations of the usefulness of case study evaluations. *Evaluation Quarterly, 3*(3), 446-459.

Wilson, T. P. (1981). A case study in qualitative research? *Social Science Information Studies, 1*(4), 241-246.

Yin, R. K. (1981). The case study as a serious research strategy. *Knowledge: Creation, Diffusion, Utilization, 3*, 97-114.

Yin, R. K. (1981). The case study crisis: Some answers. *Administrative Science Quarterly, 26*(1), 58-65.

Yin, R. K. (1989a). *Case study research: Design and method* (rev. ed.). Newbury Park, CA: Sage.

Yin, R. (1989b). Research design issues in using the case study method to study management information systems. In J. I. Cash & P. R. Lawrence (Eds.), *The information systems research challenge: Qualitative research methods* (pp. 1-6). Boston: Harvard Business School.

Yin, R. K. (1992). The case study method as a tool for doing evaluation. *Current Sociology, 40*(1), 121-137.

Yin, R. K. (in press). The role of theory in doing case study research and evaluations. In H. T. Chen & P. H. Rossi (Eds.), *Theory-driven evaluation in analyzing policies and programs*. Westport, CT: Greenwood.

Zonabend, F. (1992). The monograph in European ethnology. *Current Sociology, 40*(1), 49-54.

Case Studies and Community Studies:
Some Classic Examples

Caplow, T., Bahr, H. M., Chadwick, B. A., Hill, R., & Williamson, M. H. (1982). *Middletown families: Fifty years of change and continuity.* Minneapolis: University of Minnesota Press.

Cavan, S. (1966). *Liquor license.* Chicago: Aldine.

Cox, K. R., & Johnson, R. J. (1982). *Conflict, politics and the urban scene.* Harlow, UK: Longman.

Cressey, D. R. (Ed.). (1961). *The prison: Studies in institutional organization and change.* New York: Holt.

Gans, H. J. (1962). *The urban villagers: Group and class in the life of Italian-Americans.* New York: Free Press.

Gans, H. J. (1967). *The Levittowners: Ways of life and politics in a new suburban community.* New York: Random House.

Gouldner, A. (1954). *Patterns of industrial bureaucracy.* New York: Free Press.

Holdaway, S. (1982). *Inside the British police: A force at work.* Oxford, UK: Blackwell.

Hollinghead, A. B. (1949). *Elmtown's youth.* New York: John Wiley.

Humphreys, L. (1975). *Tearoom trade: Impersonal sex in public places* (2nd ed.). Chicago: Aldine.

Jacobs, J. B. (1977). *Stateville: The penitentiary in mass society.* Chicago: University of Chicago Press.

Jefferys, M., & Sachs, H. (1983). *Rethinking general practice: Dilemmas in primary medical care.* London: Tavistock.

Lacey, C. (1970). *Hightown grammar: The school as a social system.* Manchester, UK: Manchester University Press.

Lein, L. (1984). *Families without villains: American families in an era of change.* Lexington, MA: D. C. Heath.

Lewis, O. (1959). *Five families: Mexican case studies in the culture of poverty.* New York: Basic Books.

Lewis, O. (1969). *A death in the Sanchez family.* New York: Random House.

Lynd, R. S., & Lynd, H. M. (1929). *Middletown: A study in contemporary American culture.* New York: Harcourt, Brace.

Lynd, R. S., & Lynd, H. M. (1937). *Middletown in transition.* New York: Harcourt.

Metz, D. (1981). *Running hot: Structure and stress in ambulance work.* Cambridge, MA: Abt.

Rubinstein, J. (1974). *City police* (2nd ed.). New York: Ballantine.

Spradley, J. P., & Mann, B. J. (1975). *The cocktail waitress: Woman's work in a man's world.* New York: John Wiley.

Taub, R. P., Taylor, D. G., & Durham, J. (1984). *Paths of neighbourhood change: Race and crime in urban America.* Chicago: University of Chicago Press.

Vidich, A. J., & Bensman, J. (1958). *Small town in mass society.* Princeton, NJ: Princeton University Press.

Whyte, W. F. (1948). *Human relations in the restaurant industry.* New York: McGraw-Hill.

Whyte, W. F. (1981). *Street corner society: The social structure of an Italian slum* (3rd ed.). Chicago: University of Chicago Press.

Willis, P. E. (1977). *Learning to labour.* Westmead, UK: Saxon House.

Willis, P. E. (1978). *Profane culture.* London: Routledge & Kegan Paul.

Wylie, L. W. (1958). *Village in the Vaucluse.* Cambridge, MA: Harvard University Press.

Young, M., & Willmott, P. (1957). *Family and kinship in East London*. London: Routledge & Kegan Paul.

C. FIELDWORK

Adams, R., & Preiss, J. (1960). (Eds.). *Human organization research: Field relations and techniques*. Homewood, IL: Dorsey.

Adler, P. A., & Adler, P. (1987). *Membership roles in field research*. Newbury Park, CA: Sage.

Adler, P. A., & Rochford, E. B., Jr. (1986). The politics of participation in field research. *Urban Life, 14*(4), 363-376.

Babchuck, N. (1962). The role of the researcher as participant observer and participant as observer in the field situation. *Human Organization, 21*(3), 225-228.

Bain, R. K. (1950). The researcher's role: A case study. *Human Organization, 9*(1), 23-38.

Barker, T. L. (1988). Field research and observational studies. In T. L. Barker, *Doing social research* (pp. 228-251). New York: McGraw-Hill.

Barnes, J. A. (1963). Some ethical problems in modern field work. *British Journal of Sociology, 14*, 118-134.

Bennet, J. W. (1948). A survey of techniques and methodology in field work. *American Sociology Review, 13*, 672-689.

Bensman, J., & Vidich, A. J. (1960). Social theory in field research. *American Journal of Sociology, 65*, 577-584.

Bouchard, T. J., Jr. (1976). Field research methods. In M. D. Dunnette (Ed.), *Industrial and organizational psychology* (pp. 363-413). Chicago: Rand McNally.

Bulmer, M. (Ed.). (1982). *Social research ethics*. London: Macmillan.

Burgess, R. G. (Ed.). (1982). *Field research: A sourcebook and field manual*. London: Allen & Unwin.

Burgess, R. G. (Ed.). (1985). *Field methods in the study of education*. London: Falmer.

Campbell, D. T. (1955). The informant in qualitative research. *American Journal of Sociology, 60*, 339-342.

Cassell, J. (1978). Risk and benefit to subjects of fieldwork. *American Sociology, 13*, 134-143.

Cassell, J. (1980). Ethical principles for conducting fieldwork. *American Anthropology, 82*(1), 28-41.

Cassell, J., & Wax, M. (Ed.). (1980). Ethical problems of fieldwork. *Social Problems, 27*, 259-378.

Chapin, F. S. (1920). *Field work and social research*. New York: Century.

Christinat, J.-L. (1980). Problèmes de terrain ou l'expérience ethnographique [Fieldwork problems, or the ethnographic experience]. *Bulletin de la société suisse des Américanistes, 44*, 39-48.

Clifford, J. (1980). Fieldwork, reciprocity and the making of ethnographic texts. *Man, 15*, 518-532.

Coffield, F., & Borrill, C. (1983). Entrée and exit. *Sociology Review, 31*(3), 520-545.

Cook, T. D., & Campbell, D. T. (1979). *Quasi-experimentation: Design and analysis issues for field settings*. Chicago: Rand McNally.

66

Cordonnier, R. (Ed.). (1988). Chercheurs et informateurs [Researchers and informers; special issue]. *Bulletin de l'Association française des anthropologues, 34*(December).

Denzin, N. K. (1989). Participant observation: Varieties and strategies of the field method. In N. K. Denzin, *The research act* (3rd ed.) (pp. 156-181). Englewood Cliffs, NJ: Prentice-Hall.

Dingwall, R. (1980). Ethics and ethnography. *Sociological Review, 28*(4), 871-891.

Douglas, J. D. (1976). *Investigative social research: Individual and team field research.* Beverly Hills, CA: Sage.

Duster, T., Matza, D., & Wellman, D. (1979). Field work and the protection of human subjects. *American Sociologist, 14*(3), 136-142.

Easterday, L., Papademas, D., Schorr, L., & Valentine, C. (1977). The making of a female research: Role problems in field work. *Urban Life, 6*, 333-348.

Emerson, R. M. (1981). Observational field work. *Annual Review of Sociology, 7*, 351-378.

Emerson, R. M. (1983). *Contemporary field research.* Boston: Little, Brown.

Everhart, R. B. (1977). Between stranger and friend: Some consequences of long-term fieldwork in schools. *American Educational Research Journal, 14*(1), 1-15.

Favret-Saada, J., & Contreras, J. (1981). *Corps pour corps: Enquête sur la sorcellerie dans le Bocage* [Bewitched bodies: Studying witchcraft in the French Bocage region]. Paris: Gallimard.

Fiedler, J. (1978). *Field research: A manual for logistics and management of scientific studies in natural settings.* San Francisco: Jossey-Bass.

Gardner, B. B., & Whyte, W. F. (1946). Methods for the study of human relations in industry. *American Sociological Review, 11*, 506-512.

Garrigues, E. (1988). Le temps du terrain et le temps comme terrain [The time of the field and the time as field]. *L'Homme et la société, 4*(90), 51-62.

Gast, M., & Panoff, M. (Eds.). (1986). *L'accès au terrain en pays étranger et outre-mer* [Field access abroad]. Paris: L'Harmattan.

Geer, B. (1964). First days in the field. In P. E. Hammond (Ed.), *Sociologist at work: Essays on the craft of social research* (pp. 322-344). New York: Basic Books.

Glazer, M. (1966). Field work in an hostile environment: A chapter in the sociology of social research in Chile. *Comparative Education Review, 10*, 367-376.

Glazer, M. (1972). *The research adventure: Promise and problems of fieldwork.* New York: Random House.

Golde, P. (Ed.). (1986). *Women in the field: Anthropological experiences* (2nd ed.). Chicago: Aldine.

Grawitz, M. (1979). Les techniques vivantes [Living techniques]. In M. Grawitz, *Méthodes des sciences sociales* [Social sciences methods] (pp. 697-979). Paris: Dalloz.

Gray, P.-S. (1980). Exchange and access in field work. *Urban Life, 2*, 309-311.

Greenhouse, C.-J. (1985). Anthropology at home: Whose home? *Human Organization, 44*(3), 261-264.

Gubrium, J. (1988). *Analyzing field reality.* Newbury Park, CA: Sage.

Gubrium, J., & Silverman, D. (1989). *The politics of field research.* Newbury Park, CA: Sage.

Guiart, J. (1968). Réflexions sur la méthode en ethnologie [Observations on method in ethnology]. *Cahiers internationaux de sociologie, 45*(15), 81-98.

Gutwirth, J. (1973). Pour la méthode ethnologique [For the ethnological method]. In M. Sauter (Ed.), *L'homme, hier et aujourd'hui, recueil d'études en hommage à André Leroi-*

Gourhan [Man, then and now, collection of studies dedicated to André Leroi-Gourhan] (pp. 775-783). Paris: Cujas.

Habenstein, R. W. (Ed.). (1970). *Pathways to data: Field methods for studying ongoing social organizations.* Chicago: Aldine.

Hammersley, M., & Atkinson, P. (1983). *Ethnography: Principles in practice.* New York: Tavistock.

Heberle, R. (1982). In praise of field work: An autobiographical note. *Zeitschrift für Soziologie, 11*(2), 105-112.

Holy, L., & Stuchlik, M. (1983). *Actions, norms and representations, foundations of anthropological inquiry.* Cambridge, UK: Cambridge University Press.

Homan, R., & Bulmer, M. (Collab.). (1980). The ethics of covert methods. *British Journal of Sociology of Education, 31*(1), 46-65.

Johnson, J. M. (1975). *Doing field research.* New York: Free Press.

Jongmans, D. G., & Gutkind, P. C. (Eds.). (1967). *Anthropologist in the field.* Assen, The Netherlands: Van Gorcum.

Jorian, P. (1974). Quelques réflexions sur les conditions de l'enquête de terrain en anthropologie sociale [Some thoughts on the fieldwork conditions in social anthropology]. *Revue de l'Institut de sociologie, 4,* 619-639.

Junker, B. H. (1960). *Field work: An introduction to the social sciences.* Chicago: University of Chicago Press.

Karp, I., & Kendall, M. B. (1982). Reflexivity in field work. In P. F. Secord (Ed.), *Explaining human behavior: Consciousness, human action and social structure* (pp. 249-273). Beverly Hills, CA: Sage.

Katz, D. (1963). Les études sur le terrain [Field studies]. In L. Festinger & D. Katz (Eds.), *Les méthodes de recherche dans les sciences sociales* [Research methods in social sciences] (pp. 68-117). Paris: PUF.

Katz, J. (1983). A theory of qualitative methodology: The social system of analytic fieldwork. In R. M. Emerson (Ed.), *Contemporary field research* (pp. 127-148). Boston: Little, Brown.

Kertzer, D. I. (1978). Methods, problems and expedients of fieldwork. *Uomo, 2*(2), 151-159.

Kilani, M. (1988). L'anthropologie de terrain et le terrain de l'anthropologie: Observation, description et textualisation en anthropologie [Field anthropology and the field of anthropology: Observing, describing, and writing in anthropology]. *Travaux du Centre de Recherches Sémiologiques, 55,* 1-38.

Kourganoff, M. (1965). Les instruments d'enquête utilisés pour les études sur le terrain [Research tools for field studies]. *Revue française de sociologie, 6,* 137-147.

Lacey, C. (1976). Problems of sociological fieldwork: A review of the methodology of hightown grammar. In M. Shipman (Ed.), *The organisation and impact of social research* (pp. 63-88). London: Routledge & Kegan Paul.

Lacoste, Y. (1977). Divers problèmes à propos de l'enquête et du terrain [Some fieldwork and inquiry problems]. *Hérodote, 8,* 3-20.

Lindenfeld, J. (1984). Ethnologie urbaine et ethnographie de la communication: préliminaires à une étude sur les places marchandes [Urban ethnology and ethnography of communication: Preliminaries for a study of market places]. *Langage et société, 30,* 3-28.

Lofland, J. (1974). Styles of reporting qualitative field research. *American Sociologist, 9,* 101-111.

Lourau, R. (1986). Jeanne Favret: l'implication sur le terrain [Jeanne Favret: The field implication]. In *Marx ou pas, réflexions sur un centenaire* [Marx or not, observations on a centenarian] (pp. 80-84). Paris: Études et documentation internationales.

Lourau, R. (1988). *Le journal de recherche: Matériaux d'une théorie de l'implication* [The research diary: Material for a theory of implication]. Paris: Méridiens-Klincksieck.

Maget, M. (1953). *Guide d'étude directe des comportements culturels* [A guide for the direct study of cultural behaviors]. Paris: CNRS.

Malinowski, B. (1985). *Journal d'ethnographe* [Diary of an ethnographist]. Paris: Seuil. (Coll. Recherches anthropologiques)

Mayoni, J. R. (1983). Eager visitor, reluctant host: The anthropologist as stranger. *Anthropologia, 25*(2), 221-249.

Mead, M. (1933). More comprehensive field methods. *American Anthropologist, 35,* 1-15.

Mo, L. (1979). Is field work scientific? *Munich Social Science Review, 1,* 5-17.

Monjardet, D. (1982). Terrain et théorie: faut-il se garder de mettre les pieds dans l'entreprise [Field and theory: Must we keep from setting foot in the company investigated]. *Sociologie du Sud-est, 33-34,* 21-30.

Montandon, C. (1983). Problèmes éthiques de la recherche en sciences sociales: le cas d'une étude en milieu carcéral [Ethical problems in social sciences research: The case of a study in a penal context]. *Revue suisse de sociologie, 9*(2), 215-233.

Murphy, J.-W. (1983). Qualitative methodology, hypothesis testing and the needs assessment. *Journal of Sociology and Social Welfare, 10*(1), 136-147.

Murphy, M. D. (1985). Rumors of identity: Gossip and report in ethnographic research. *Human Organization, 44*(2), 132-137.

Newbold, A. R. (1981). Ethical principles in anthropological research: One or many? *Human Organization, 40*(2), 155-160.

Newby, H. (1977). In the field: Reflections on the study of Suffolk farm workers. In C. Bell & H. Newby (Eds.), *Doing sociological research* (pp. 108-129). London: Allen & Unwin.

O'Kane, F. (1981). Gens de la terre, gens du discours: terrain, méthode et réflexion dans l'étude d'une communauté de montagne et de ses émigrés [People of the land, people of speech: Field, method, and reflections in the study of a community of mountain dwellers and its emigrants]. *Information S.E.G./S.S.E., 2,* 3-5.

Paoli-Elzingre, M. (1987). Questions de terrain. Qu'est-ce que je fais quand je suis sociologue? [Field questions: What am I to do if I'm a sociologist?]. In D. Lecoq & J.-L. Lory (Eds.), *Écrits d'ailleurs: Georges Bataille et les ethnologues* [Writings from elsewhere: George Bataille and the ethnologists] (pp. 75-81). Paris: Éditions de la Maison des sciences de l'homme.

Pelto, P. J., & Pelto, G. H. (1978). Ethnography: The fieldwork enterprise. In J. J. Honigmann (Ed.), *Handbook of social and cultural anthropology* (pp. 241-288). Chicago: Rand McNally.

Peneff, J. (1985). Reflexions: Fieldwork in Algeria. *Qualitative Sociology, 8,* 65-78.

Petonnet, C. (1973). Méthodologie ethnologique en milieu urbain: un groupe espagnol [Ethnological methodology in an urban context: A Spanish group]. In M. Sauter (Ed.), *L'homme, hier et aujourd'hui, recueil d'études en hommage à André Leroi-Gourhan* [Man, then and now, collection of studies dedicated to André Leroi-Gourhan] (pp. 457-468). Paris: Cujas.

69

Pettigrew, A. M. (1990). Longitudinal field research on change: Theory and practice. *Organization Science, 1*(3), 267-292.

Powdermaker, H. (1967). *Stranger and friend: The way of an anthropologist.* New York: Norton.

Powdermaker, H. (1968). Field work. In *International encyclopedia of the social sciences* (Vol. 5, pp. 418-424). London: Collier-Macmillan.

Pulman, B. (1986). Le débat anthropologie/psychanalyse et la référence au terrain [The anthropology/psychoanalysis debate and its reference to the idea of field]. *Cahiers internationaux de sociologie, 80*(January-June), 5-26.

Punch, M. (1986). *The politics and ethics of fieldwork.* Beverly Hills, CA: Sage.

Queloz, N. (1984). La notion de terrain et le recueil des données en sociologie [The idea of field and data gathering in sociology]. *Cahiers de l'ISSP, 5*(September), 121-135.

Rabinow, P. (1977). *Reflections on fieldwork in Morocco.* Berkeley: University of California Press.

Ramognino, N. (1992). L'observation, un résumé de la réalité [Observation, reality summarized]. *Current Sociology, 40*(1), 55-75.

Rose, D. (1987). On the ethnographic touch. *Dialectical Anthropology, 12*(1), 105-124.

Roue, M.-M. (1984). Rock'n roll et ethnologie: une question de méthode [Rock'n roll and ethnology: A methodological question]. *Raison présente, 69,* 43-55.

Rynkiewich, M. A., & Spradley, J. P. (Eds.). (1976). *Ethics and anthropology: Dilemmas in fieldwork.* New York: John Wiley.

Salamone, F. A. (1979). Epistemological implications of fieldwork and their consequences. *American Anthropologist, 81,* 46-60.

Schatzman, L., & Strauss, A. (1973). *Field research: Strategies for a natural sociology.* Englewood Cliffs, NJ: Prentice Hall.

Schein, E. H. (1987). *The clinical perspective in fieldwork.* Newbury Park, CA: Sage.

Scott, R. W. (1963). Field work in a formal organization: Some dilemmas in the role of observer. *Human Organization, 22*(2), 162-168.

Shaffir, W. B. (1985). Some reflections on approaches to fieldwork in Hassidic communities. *Jewish Journal of Sociology, 27*(2), 115-134.

Shaffir, W. B., Stebbins, R. A., & Turowetz, A. (Eds.). (1980). *Fieldwork experience: Qualitative approach to social research.* New York: St. Martins.

Sieber, S. D. (1973). The integration of fieldwork and survey methods. *American Journal of Sociology, 78,* 1335-1359.

Smith, C. D., & Kornblum, W. (Eds.). (1989). *In the field: Research on the field research experience.* New York: Praeger.

Soudière, M. de la. (1988). L'inconfort du terrain [Uncomfortable fieldwork]. *Terrain, 11*(November), 94-105.

Srinivas, M.-N., Shah, A.-M., & Ramas-Wamy, E.-A. (Eds.). (1979). *The fieldworker and the field: Problems and challenges in sociological investigations.* Delhi: Oxford University Press.

Stocking, G. W., Jr. (Ed.). (1983). *Observers observed: Essays in ethnographic fieldwork.* Madison: Wisconsin University Press.

Stoddart, K. (1986). The presentation of everyday life: Some textual strategies for "adequate ethnography." *Urban Life, 15,* 103-121.

Styles, J. (1979). Outsider/insider: Researching gay baths. *Urban Life, 8,* 135-152.

Taylor, S., & Bodgan, R. (1981). A qualitative approach to community adjustment. In R. H. Bruininks, C. E. Meyers, B. B. Sigford, & K. C. Larkin (Eds.), *De-institutionalization and community adjustment of mentally retarded people*. Washington, DC: American Association on Mental Deficiency.

Trice, H. M. (1956). The outsider's role in field study. *Sociology and Social Research, 41*(1), 27-32.

Turner, W. H. (1986). The black ethnographer: "At home" in Harlan: A commentary and research reponse to Stephenson and Greer. *Human Organization, 45*(3), 279-282.

Vidich, A., & Bensman, J. (1954). The validity of field data. *Human Organization, 13*(1), 20-27.

Warren, C.A.B. (1988). *Gender issues in field research*. Newbury Park, CA: Sage.

Warren, C.A.B., & Rasmussen, P. K. (1977). Sex and gender in field research. *Urban Life, 6*, 349-370.

Wax, R. (1957). Twelve years later: An analysis of field experience. *American Journal of Sociology, 63*, 133-142.

Wax, R. (1971). *Doing fieldwork: Warnings and advice*. Chicago: University of Chicago Press.

Weber, R. (1987). Une pédagogie collective de l'enquête de terrain [A collective way of teaching fieldwork]. *Études rurales, 107-108*(July-December), 243-249.

Werner, O., & Schoepfle, M. G. (1987). *Systematic fieldwork: Vol. 1. Foundations of ethnography and interviewing; Vol. 2. Ethnographic analysis and data management*. Newbury Park, CA: Sage.

Williams, T. R. (1967). *Field methods in the study of culture*. New York: Holt, Rinehart & Winston.

Young, P. V. (1966). Field observation in social research. In *Scientific social surveys and research* (4th ed.). Englewood Cliffs, NJ: Prentice-Hall.

Zelditch, M. (1962). Some methodological problems of field studies. *American Journal of Sociology, 67*, 566-576.

D. ON THE MICRO/MACRO DISTINCTION: LOCAL VERSUS GLOBAL

Alexander, J., Giesen, B., Munch, R., & Smelser, N. J. (Eds.). (1987). *The micro-macro link*. Berkeley: University of California Press.

Barbichon, G. (1989). Culture et universalité du particulier [The culture and universality of the particular]. In M. Segalen (Ed.), *L'autre et le semblable* [The other and the same] (pp. 159-182). Paris: CNRS.

Bradshaw, Y., & Wallace, M. (1991). Informing generality and explaining uniqueness: The place of case studies in comparative research. *International Journal of Comparative Sociology, 32*(1-2), 154-171.

Bromberger, C. (1987). Du grand au petit: Variations des échelles et des objets d'analyse dans l'histoire récente de l'ethnologie de la France [From big to small: Varying scales and objects under analysis in France's recent ethnology history]. In I. Chiva & U. Jeggle (Eds.), *Ethnologie en miroir: la France et les pays de langue allemande* [The reflections of ethnology: France and the German-speaking countries] (pp. 67-94). Paris: Éditions de la Maison des Sciences de l'Homme.

Canguilhem, G. (1968). Du singulier à la singularité en épistémologie biologique [From singular to singularity in biological epistemology]. In G. Canguilhem, *Études d'histoire et de philosophie des sciences* [Studies in history and philosophy of sciences] (pp. 211-225). Paris: Vrin.

Castel, L. R. (1989). Institutions totales et configurations ponctuelles [Total institutions and punctual configurations]. In I. Joseph (Ed.), *Le parler frais d'Erving Goffman* [The untainted speech of Erving Goffman] (pp. 31-44). Paris: Les Éditions de Minuit.

Collins, R. (1983). Micromethods as a basis for macrosociology. *Urban Life, 12*, 184-202.

Collins, R. (1986). On the micro-foundations of macro-sociology. *American Journal of Sociology, 91*, 1336-1355.

Collins, R. (1988). The micro contribution to macro sociology, *Sociological Theory, 6*(2), 242-253.

Collins, R. (1992). The romanticism of agency/structure versus the analysis of micro/macro. *Current Sociology, 40*(1), 77-97.

Cornaert, M., & Saint-Blancat, C. (1988). Le local et la contemporanéité: interférences micro et macro-sociologiques [Locality and topicality: Micro and macro sociological interferences]. *Espaces et Sociétés, 4-5*, 277-291.

Couty, P. (1984). La vérité doit être construite [Truth must be constructed]. *Les cahiers de l'ORSTOM, 20*(1), 5-15.

Davidson, P. O., & Costello, G. G. (1969). *N = 1: Experimental studies of single cases.* New York: Van Nostrand Reinhold.

Decoster, M. (1985). Lois, modèles et déterminisme sociologiques [Laws, models, and determinism in sociology]. *Revue de l'Institut de sociologie, 1-2*, 191-206.

Dewalt, B. R., & Pelto, P. J. (1985). *Micro and macro levels of analysis in anthropology: Issues in theory and research.* London: Westriew Press.

Dukes, W. F. (1965). N = 1. *Psychological Bulletin, 64*(1), 74-79.

Eisenstadt, S. N., & Helle, H. J. (Eds.). (1985). *Perspectives on sociological theory: Vol. 1. Macro-sociological theory; Vol. 2. Micro-sociological theory.* Beverly Hills, CA: Sage.

Ferrarotti, F. (1983). La biographie comme interaction [Biography as interaction] and La socialité de l'individu [The social life of the individual]. In F. Ferrarotti, *Histoire et histoires de vie* [History and life stories]. (pp. 47-58, 59-65). Paris: Librairie des Méridiens.

Fine, G. A. (1988). *On the macro foundations of microsociology: Meaning, order and comparative context.* Minneapolis: University of Minnesota, Department of Sociology.

Geertz, C. (1983). *Local knowledge: Further essays in interpretative anthropology.* New York: Basic Books.

Giddens, A. (1984a). Against "micro" and "macro": Social and system integration. In A. Giddens, *The constitution of society* (pp. 139-145). Berkeley: University of California Press.

Ginzburg, C. (1982). *The cheese and the worms* (J. & A. Tedeschi, Trans.). London: Routledge & Kegan Paul. (Original work published 1976, *Il formaggio e i vermi: Il cosmo di un mugnaio del '500.* Italy: Giulio Einaudi editore.)

Ginzburg, C., & Poni, C. (1989). La micro histoire [Micro history]. In A. Jacob (Ed.), *L'univers philosophique* [The philosophical universe] (Vol. 1, pp. 1316-1319). Paris: PUF.

Gulick, J. (1984). The essence of urban anthropology: Integration of micro and macro research perspectives. *Urban Anthropology, 13*(2-3), 295-306.

Hamel, J. (1992). On the status of singularity in sociology. *Current Sociology, 40*(1), 99-119.

Hammersley, M. (1984). Interpretative sociology and the macro-micro problem [mimeo copy]. In *Conflict and change in education: A sociological perspective*. Philadelphia, PA: Unit 16, Open University Course E205, Milton Keynes, Open University.

Hargreaves, A. The micro-macro problem in the sociology of education. In R. G. Burgess (Ed.), *Issues in educational research: Qualitative methods* (pp. 21-47). London: Falmer.

Holt, R. R. (1962). Individuality and generalization in the psychology of personality. *Journal of Personality, 30*, 377-404.

Javeau, C. (1989). Singularité et sociologie [Singularity and sociology]. *Société, 6*(Fall), 229-241.

Kemeny, J. (1976). Perspectives on the micro-macro distinction. *Sociological Review, 24*(4), 731-752.

Kennedy, M. M. (1976). Generalizing from single case studies. *Evaluation Quarterly, 3*, 661-678.

Kilani, M. (1989). Une définition de l'anthropologie: l'articulation du local et du global [A definition of anthropology: The micro and macro link]. In M. Kilani, *Introduction à l'anthropologie* [An introduction to anthropology] (pp. 33-40). Switzerland: Éditions Payot Lausanne.

Knorr-Cetina, K., & Cicourel, A. C. (Eds.). (1981). *Advances in social theory and methodology: Toward an integration of micro- and macro-sociologies*. Boston: Routledge & Kegan Paul.

Kratochwill, T. R. (1978). *Single subject research*. New York: Academic Press.

Lawler, E. J., Ridgeway, C., & Markovsky, B. (1989). *Structural social psychology and micro-macro linkages*. Iowa City: University of Iowa, Department of Sociology.

Miguelez, R. (1984). L'articulation du général et du particulier: une approche méthodologique dans le champ des sciences sociales [The micro and macro link: A methodological approach in social sciences]. *Philosophiques, 11*(2), 251-275.

Miller, D. L. (1982). Ritual in the work of Durkheim and Goffman: The link between the macro and the micro. *Humanity and Society, 6*(2), 122-134.

Ross, F. A. (1931). On generalisation from limited social data. *Social Forces, 10*, 32-37.

Scheff, T. (1990). *Microsociology: Discourse, emotion and social structure*. Chicago: University of Chicago Press.

Schegloff, E. A. (1987). Between macro and micro: Contexts and other connections. In J. C. Alexander (Ed.), *The micro-macro link* (pp. 207-234). Berkeley: University of California Press.

Stouffer, S. A. (1941). Notes on the case-study and the unique case. *Sociometry, 4*, 349-357.

Stouffer, S. A., & Lazarsfeld, P. F. (1937). Notes on the logic of generalisation in family case studies. *Research memorandum on the family in the Depression*. New York: Social Science Research Council.

Turner, J. H. (1983). Theoretical strategies for linking micro and macro processes: An evaluation of seven approaches in macro-micro linkages. *Western Sociological Review Logan, 14*(1), 4-15.

Wiley, N. (1988). The micro-macro problem in social theory. *Sociological Theory, 6*(2), 254-261.

Yogev, A., & Archer, M., et al. (1987). Linking micro and macro perspectives in the sociology of education. *Revue internationale de sociologie, 23*(1).

E. DESCRIPTION: PROBLEMS AND METHODS

Theoretical and Methodological Aspects

Bernier, L., & Perrault, I. (1985). *L'artiste et l'oeuvre à faire* [The artist and his work to be]. Québec: IQRC.

Den Hollander, A.N.J. (1967). Social description: The problem of reliability and validity. In D. G. Longmans & P.C.W. Gutkind (Eds.), *Anthropologist in the field* (pp. 1-34). Assen, The Netherlands: Van Gorcum.

Denzin, N. K. (1989). Thick description. In N. K. Denzin, *Interpretative interactionism* (pp. 83-103). Newbury Park, CA: Sage.

Granger, G.-G. (1979). Théorie et expérience [Theory and experience]. In J. de la Campagne (Ed.), *Philosopher* [Philosophizing] (pp. 341-351). Paris: Seuil.

Hammersley, M. (1990). What's wrong with ethnography? The myth of theoretical description. *Sociology, 24*(4), 597-615.

Houle, G. (1986). Histoires et récits de vie: la redécouverte obligée du sens commun [Life stories: The compelling rediscovery of common sense]. In D. Desmarais & P. Grell (Eds.), *Les récits de vie* [Life stories] (pp. 35-51). Montréal: Éditions Saint-Martin.

Krishnarao, B. (1961). The descriptive method in social research. *Sociologia Bulletin, 10*(2), 46-52.

Loubet del Bayle, J.-L. (1986). La description [Description]. In J.-L. Loubet del Bayle, *Introduction aux méthodes des sciences sociales* [An introduction to social science's methods] (pp. 124-146). Toulouse: Privat.

Matalon, B. (1988). Les descriptions [Descriptions]. In B. Matalon, *Décrire, expliquer, prévoir* [Describe, explain, forecast] (pp. 105-120). Paris: Armand Colin.

Pharo, P. (1985). Problèmes empiriques de la sociologie compréhensive [Empirical problems of comprehensive sociology]. *Revue française de sociologie, 26*(1), 120-149.

Quéré, L. (Ed.). (1985). *La description, un impératif?* [Description, a must do?] (2 vols.). Paris: Centre d'étude des mouvements sociaux, EHESS.

Quéré, L. (1989). La vie sociale est une scène [Social life as a stage]. In I. Joseph (Ed.), *Le parler frais d'Erving Goffman* [The untainted speech of Erving Goffman] (pp. 47-82). Paris: Les Éditions de Minuit.

Sacks, J. (1963). Sociological description. *Berkeley Journal of Sociology, 8*(13), 1-17.

Smith, D. E. (1981). On sociological description: A method from Marx. *Human Studies, 4*(4), 313-337.

Constructing the Explanation

Balandier, G. (1956). L'expérience de l'ethnologue et le problème de l'explication [The ethnologist's experience and the explanation problem]. *Cahiers internationaux de sociologie, 21*(July-December), 114-127.

Bawin-Legros, B. (1982). Du type d'explication possible au choix d'une méthode réelle: le cas particulier de la mobilité sociale des femmes à travers le récit d'une recherche [From the possible type of explanation to the selection of an actual method: The case of women's social mobility as seen through the account of a research]. *Sociologie et sociétés, 14*(1), 53-63.

74

Brown, R. (1963). *Explanation in social science*. London: Routledge & Kegan Paul.

Bulmer, M. (1979). Concepts in the analysis of the qualitative data. *Sociological Review, 27*(4), 651-679.

Burgess, E. W. (1929). Is prediction feasible in social work? *Social Forces, 7,* 533-545.

Cottrell, L. S. (1941). The case-study method in prediction. *Sociometry, 4,* 848-870.

Dallmayr, F., & McCarthy, T. A. (Eds.). (1977). *Understanding and social inquiry.* Notre Dame, IN: University of Notre Dame Press.

Descola, P. (1988). L'explication causale [Causal explanation]. In *Les idées de l'anthropologie* [The ideas of anthropology] (pp. 11-59). Paris: Armand Colin.

Diesing, P. (1972). *Patterns of discovery in the social sciences.* London: Routledge & Kegan Paul.

Girod, R. (1956). Le passage de la description à l'explication dans le cadre de la sociologie concrète [The passage from description to explanation in concrete sociology]. *Cahiers internationaux de sociologie, 21,* 100-113.

Granger, G.-G. (1973). L'explication dans les sciences sociales [Explanation in social sciences]. In *L'explication dans les sciences* [Explanation in sciences] (pp. 147-165). Paris: Flammarion.

Grenier, L. (1983). Sous la rubrique des objets perdus, une réflexion méthodologique sur le racisme [In the lost and found category, a methodological reflection on racism]. *Sociologie et sociétés, 15*(2), 147-153.

Gurvitch, G. (1956). La crise de l'explication en sociologie [The explanation crisis in sociology]. *Cahiers internationaux de sociologie, 21,* 3-18.

Miguelez, R. (1969). L'explication en ethnologie [Explanation in ethnology]. *Information sur les sciences sociales, 8*(3), 27-58.

Miles, M. B. (1979). Qualitative data as an attractive nuisance: The problem of analysis. *Administrative Science Quarterly, 24*(4), 590-601.

Moeckli, G. (1964). L'explication dans les sciences sociales [Explanation in social sciences]. *Cahiers Vilfredo Pareto, 3,* 29-60.

Noblit, G. W., & Hare, R. D. (1988). *Meta-ethnography: Synthesizing qualitative studies.* Newbury Park, CA: Sage.

Piaget, J. (1967). L'explication sociologique [Sociological explanation]. In J. Piaget, *Études sociologiques* (pp. 15-99). Genève: Droz.

Pirès, A. P. (1989). Analyse causale et récits de vie [Causal analysis and life stories]. *Anthropologie et sociétés, 13*(3), 37-58.

Quéré, L. (1992). Le tournant descriptif en sociologie [The descriptive turn in sociology]. *Current Sociology, 40*(1), 139-165.

Ramognino, N. (1982). Pour une approche dialectique en sociologie [For a dialectic approach in sociology]. *Sociologie et sociétés, 14*(1), 83-95.

van Parijs, P. (1977). La syntaxe de l'explication dans les sciences sociales [The explanation's syntax in social sciences]. *Recherches sociologiques, 7*(2), 211-244.

Von Wright, G. H. (1971). *Explanation and understanding*. London: Routledge & Kegan Paul.

The Style of Description: Problems in Writing Case Studies

Becker, H. S., & Richards, P. (1986). *Writing for social scientist: How to start and finish your thesis, book or article.* Chicago: University of Chicago Press.

Bertaux, D. (1979). Écrire la sociologie [Writing sociology]. *Information sur les sciences sociales, 18*(1), 7-25.

Brown, R. (1977). *A poetic for sociology: Toward a logic of discovery for the human sciences.* New York: Cambridge University Press.

Certeau, M. de. (1975). L'écriture de l'histoire [Writing history]. Paris: Gallimard.

Clifford, J. (1985). De l'ethnologue comme fiction: Conrad et Malinowski [The ethnologist as fiction: Conrad and Malinowski]. *Études rurales, 97-98,* 47-67.

Clifford, J., & Marcus, G. (1986). *Writing culture.* Berkeley: University of California Press.

Gibbal, J.-M. (1987). De l'expérience à la fiction [From experiment to fiction]. *Cahiers de sociologie économique et culturelle, 7,* 11-18.

Grataloup, N. (1990). L'écriture théorique [Theoretical writing]. *La Pensée, 274*(March-April), 47-61.

Green, B. S. (1988). *Literary methods and sociological theory: Case-studies of Simmel and Weber.* Chicago: University of Chicago Press.

Jamin, J. (1985). Le texte ethnographique: Argument [The ethnographic text: An argument]. *Études rurales, 97-98*(January-June), 13-24.

Krieger, S. (1979). Research and the construction of a text. In N. K. Denzin (Ed.), *Studies in symbolic interaction* (Vol. 2, pp. 167-187). Greenwich, CT: JAI.

McCartney, J. O. (1970). On being scientific: Changing styles of presentation of sociological research. *American Sociologist, 5,* 30-35.

Perrot, M., & Soudière, M. de la. (1988). Le masque ou la plume? Les enjeux de l'écriture en sciences sociales [The mask or the pen? The stakes of writing in social sciences]. *Information sur les sciences sociales, 27*(3), 439-460.

Simons, H. (Ed.). (1988). *Rhetoric in human sciences.* Newbury Park, CA: Sage.

Van Maanen, J. (1988). *Tales of the field: On writing ethnography.* Chicago: University of Chicago Press.

Vidal, D. (1983). La sociologie et son écriture [Sociology and its writing]. In L. Quéré (Ed.), *Problèmes d'épistémologie des sciences sociales* [Epistemological problems in social sciences] (pp. 34-47). Paris: Centre d'étude des mouvements sociaux.

F. SUPPLEMENT

Bertaux, D. (1981). *Biography and society.* Beverly Hills, CA: Sage.

Bourdieu, P. (1992). *Réponses* [Answers]. Paris: Seuil.

Bryant, C.G.A. (1985). *Positivism in social theory and research.* London: Macmillan.

Cheysson, E. (1887, May 15). La monographie d'atelier et les sociétés d'économie sociale [Workshop monograph and social economy societies]. *La Réforme Sociale.*

Falardeau, J.-C. (1968). Esquisse de ses travaux [A sketch of his work]. In L. Gérin, *L'habitant de Saint-Justin* [St. Justin's peasants] (pp. 17-48). Montréal: Presses de l'Université de Montréal.

Giddens, A. (1984b). *The constitution of society.* Berkeley: University of California Press.

Godelier, M. (1972). *Rationality and irrationality in economics.* London: NLB.

Godelier, M. (1978). La part idéelle du réel: Essai sur l'idéologique [The imagined part of reality: An essay on ideological thought]. *L'Homme, 18*(3-4), 155-188.

Godelier, M. (1980). Le marxisme dans les sciences humaines [Marxism in social sciences]. *Raison présente, 55,* 105-118.

Godelier, M. (Ed.). (1982). *Les sciences de l'homme et de la société en France* [Social sciences in France]. Paris: La Documentation française.

Godelier, M. (1984). *L'idéel et le matériel* [Imagined and material reality]. Paris: Fayard.

Granger, G.-G. (1986). Pour une épistémologie du travail scientifique [An epistemology of scientific work]. In J. Hamburger (Ed.), *La philosophie des sciences aujourd'hui* [The philosophy of sciences today] (pp. 111-122). Paris: Gauthier-Villars.

Granger, G.-G. (1988). *Pour la connaissance philosophique* [For philosophical knowledge]. Paris: Odile Jacob.

Granger, G.-G. (1989). Peut-on assigner des frontières à la connaissance scientifique [Can we surmise the limits of scientific knowledge?]. In R. Bouveresse (Ed.), *Karl Popper et la science aujourd'hui* [Karl Popper and today's science] (pp. 9-19). Paris: Aubier.

Jacob, P. (1989). Présentation [Presentation]. In P. Jacob (Ed.), *Epistémologie: L'Age de la science* [Epistemology: The age of science] (Vol. 2, pp. 9-17). Paris: Odile Jacob.

Leach, E. (1964). *Political systems of Highland Burma.* London: G. Bell & Sons.

Malinowski, B. (1953). *Argonauts of the Western Pacific.* London: Routledge & Kegan Paul. (Original work published 1922)

Marc-Lipiansky, M. (1973). *Le structuralisme de Lévi-Strauss* [Lévi-Strauss's structuralism]. Paris: Payot.

Petitot, J. (1977). Entretien avec René Thom [A conversation with René Thom]. *Mathématiques et sciences humaines, 15*(59), 27-38.

Pirès, A. P. (1982). La méthode qualitative en Amérique du Nord: un débat manqué (1918-1960) [Qualitative method in North America: A debate that failed (1918-1960)]. *Sociologie et sociétés, 14*(1), 15-29.

Poupart, J., Rains, P., & Pirès, A. (1983). Les méthodes qualitatives et la sociologie américaine [Qualitative methods and American sociology]. *Déviance et société, 7*(1), 63-91.

Sales, A. (1979). *La bourgeoisie industrielle au Québec* [The industrial middle-class in Quebec]. Montréal: Presses de l'Université de Montréal.

Stouffer, S. A. (1931). Experimental comparison of a statistical and a case history technique of attitude research. *Publications of the American Sociological Society, 25,* 154-156.

Strauss, A., & Glaser, B. (1967). *The discovery of grounded theory: Strategies for qualitative research.* Chicago: Aldine.

Thom, R. (1975). *Structural stability and morphogenesis: An outline of a general theory of models.* Reading, MA: W. A. Benjamin.

Thom, R. (1983). *Paraboles et catastrophes* [Parabolas and catastrophes]. Paris: Flammarion.

ABOUT THE AUTHORS

JACQUES HAMEL is a full Professor in the Sociology Department of the Université de Montréal. He teaches methodology and epistemology, as well as the theories of culture, knowledge, and ideology in undergraduate, graduate, and postgraduate seminars.

For several years, his research has focused on qualitative methodology, in particular on the case method in sociology, which he pursues by means of grants from the Social Sciences and Humanities Research Council of Canada. He has published a number of articles on the subject in international journals such as *International Social Science Journal, Cahiers internationaux de sociologie*, and *Anthropologie et sociétés*. He recently supervised the publication of an issue of *Current Sociology* devoted to the case study in sociology. In addition, he has published an important article on "the status of singularity in the exact sciences and in the social sciences" in the UNESCO journal *Diogenes*. He is also conducting research on the sociological theory of transition with a view to studying the Francophone economy in Quebec. These studies are pursued within the framework of an international team grouped under the auspices of the Social Anthropology Laboratory of the Collège de France. Lastly, he has recently undertaken investigations on the "baby boom" and "baby bust" generations.

Jacques Hamel has benefited, for the purpose of this study, from the collaboration of **STÉPHANE DUFOUR** and **DOMINIC FORTIN**, who are research assistants in the Sociology Department of the Université de Montréal.